Savoir Faire

1,000+ Foreign Words & Phrases You Should Know to Sound Smart

- Laura Lee -

To all of my foreign language teachers:

Merci. Danke. Gratias tibi ago.

And to Valery Lantratov, spasibo.

Savoir Faire

Quarto is the authority on a wide range of topics.

Quarto educates, entertains and enriches the lives of our readers—enthusiasts and lovers of hands-on living.

www.quartoknows.com

First published in the United States of America in 2016 by
Wellfleet Press, a member of
Quarto Publishing Group USA Inc.
142 West 36th Street, 4th Floor
New York, New York 10018
quartoknows.com
Visit our blogs at quartoknows.com

10 9 8 7 6 5 4 3 2 1

ISBN: 978-1-57715-125-8

Cover Design and Page Layout: Ashley Prine, Tandem Books
Editor: Katherine Furman, Tandem Books
Cover Illustration and Page Borders: © swiejko/Creative Market

Printed in China

INTRODUCTION

I'VE HAD A FASCINATION WITH FOREIGN LANGUAGES since I was a kid watching segments on *Sesame Street* in English and Spanish. I grew up in metro Detroit, near the Canadian border. As soon as the U.S. version of *Sesame Street* was finished, I could switch over to the Canadian channel and watch a version with segments in French. I somewhat randomly chose French as my foreign language in high school and that is how I ended up as an exchange student living outside Paris.

One of my classes at the Lycée de Pontoise was Latin. I word it this passive way because it would be a bald-faced lie to say I "learned" Latin or even that I "studied" it. I would like to have mastered Latin (Italian, French, Spanish, and Portuguese are more or less just Latin spelled badly), but I was confronted with a major obstacle to learning it: I was being taught it in French.

When you learn a living language, like French, you begin with quotidian phrases like "Can you please direct me to the train station?" When you study a dead language, like Latin, they start your instruction with phrases like "The knights conquered valiantly," and "All of Gaul is divided into three parts." I did not even know how to say these things in French!

I was doomed to fail my French-Latin class, but my kind instructor gave me an A for effort and passed me anyway.

I took away three things from my Latin class:

1. Latin is hard.
2. No one knows how it was pronounced. The accepted pronunciation of a Latin term uttered by a French speaker will sound French. It will be a bit more Germanic to a German speaker and Russian to a Russian.
3. Those Romans really got around.

In Europe you encounter several languages on an almost daily basis. When I returned to America, I felt a bit illiterate with my one and a half languages, so I decided to study German. I had the option at my high school of studying Russian, but I made the reasonable assumption that I would never use it. This was a mistake. I did not know then that I would one day end up working with Russian ballet dancers, and becoming partners with a Muscovite. My first second language is now Russian (along with a hefty dose of French ballet terminology). Now I can ask for directions to the train station in four languages (including English), and understand the response in at least three. I can still converse about Roman emperors and the divisions of the landmass once known as Gaul in only one.

If you want to understand relatively new English words, however, there is hardly a better combination of foreign languages to study than French-Latin-German. Our mother tongue came to Britain by way of Germanic tribes—the Angles, Saxons, and Jutes. These warring ancestors were eventually converted to Christianity, and their language was augmented by the religion's Latin and Greek texts.

The English language (named for the Angles) nearly died out when the Vikings took over most of the English-speaking kingdoms in Britain between 793 and 878. In 1066, the island was conquered by French-speaking Normans, and for almost three hundred years, England had a French-speaking monarchy. English would not be used again by a British king in official documents until Henry V in 1415.

Most words in English have near synonyms with slightly different nuances dating back to the social classes of Norman times. English was the language of the peasants. (Henry V's predecessor, Edward III, only knew enough English to swear in it.) French was the language of the aristocracy, and Latin the language of scholars. So today a word with an Anglo-Saxon root sounds simple and earthy, a French synonym sounds a bit more elevated and classy, and a similar word with a Latin root sounds scholarly. For example, Saxons would say *king*, the French have a *monarch*, and the Latins had a *regent*. These days, lawyers drop Latin; upscale hoteliers drop French.

Thanks to a long history of being the underdog, English became an incredible borrowing language and has one of the largest vocabularies of any language. The *Oxford English Dictionary* lists about 500,000 words. German, by comparison, is estimated to have a vocabulary of about 185,000 words, and French less than 100,000.

English is also the great linguistic comeback kid. These days it is the *lingua franca* for business, popular culture, and international communications. And after centuries of taking terms from many languages, it is now more often a lender than a borrower, giving the French words like "le weekend" and "les blue-jeans." Linguistic purists across the world fret about hybrid languages they call "Spanglish" or "Russlish." Non-native speakers of English are believed to outnumber native speakers by a ratio of three-to-one, and "OK" is the most popular word in the world.

The words and phrases we borrow are time capsules containing entire histories of contact between cultures. By looking at the borrowings from a language as a group, you get a sense of the cultural stereotypes English speakers held about their various neighbors. French is cultured. Yiddish is funny. Spanish is macho. Italian is musical. Greek is scholarly. German is strong and serious. Asian is spiritual, giving us words for religious concepts, meditation techniques, martial arts, and alternative medicine.

It is estimated that 80 percent of English was borrowed from foreign languages. Anglo-Saxon is still its backbone, and the one hundred most frequently used words are from the ancient mother tongue (examples: the, is, you, here, there), but the bulk of our everyday speech is filled with words from other European languages. With such a rich foreign vocabulary, this could be a very thick book. So for our purposes, I have limited the entries to words that retain their foreign character—words that are used more or less as they were used in their home countries and which strike the listener as being from another tongue.

I did not include words that were borrowed from other languages in a changed form. I also decided not to include food words, so no burritos, borscht, kimchi, or sashimi. I also left out (with only a couple of exceptions) words that are derived from personal names or places.

It is a historical truism that when two peoples meet, the group with less power will have a greater incentive to learn the ways and the words of the other. The colonizers often can't be bothered. So our language retains more fossils from trading partners and warring partners than, say, the indigenous residents of the landmasses our English-speaking predecessors claimed as their own.

I was hindered by this ancestral hubris when trying to track down the histories of words of African origin. Africa is the second-largest continent in the world. It currently has fifty-four nations and there are more than one thousand languages spoken there. Europeans have historically been fairly uninterested in these distinctions. The handful of English words that do come from the African continent therefore often have murky origins. If I could not track down an etymology more specific than "African" or "probably African," I did not include the word.

When borrowing from foreign languages, there is always a question as to whether or not to follow the grammar rules of the original language or the borrowing language. For example, in German, nouns are capitalized. I made the choice to follow our own grammar rules and not to capitalize them. If you're looking for a term from French that begins with "la" or "le" they will not be alphabetized by these articles but by the first letter of the word that comes after them.

And so without further ado, I hope this collection of *bons mots* will add some *joie* to your *vivre*.

PRONUNCIATION GUIDE

VOWELS

SYMBOL	AS IN
a	c<u>a</u>p, fl<u>a</u>t
ah	f<u>a</u>ther, sch<u>o</u>lar
aw	p<u>aw</u>, fl<u>aw</u>
ey	h<u>ey</u>, t<u>a</u>pe, <u>ai</u>m, w<u>ei</u>ght
e	p<u>e</u>t, st<u>e</u>p
ee	f<u>ee</u>t, dec<u>ei</u>t
i	p<u>i</u>t, f<u>i</u>ll
eye	f<u>i</u>le, r<u>igh</u>t, wh<u>y</u>
o	p<u>o</u>t, t<u>o</u>p
oh	t<u>oe</u>, b<u>oa</u>t, r<u>o</u>pe
ow	c<u>ow</u>, cl<u>ou</u>d
oy	b<u>oy</u>, b<u>oi</u>l
u	c<u>u</u>p, t<u>o</u>n, fl<u>oo</u>d
oo	b<u>oo</u>t, s<u>ui</u>t

CONSONANTS

SYMBOL	AS IN
b	<u>b</u>at, ca<u>b</u>
ch	<u>ch</u>ip, pi<u>tch</u>
d	<u>d</u>og, go<u>d</u>
f	<u>f</u>all, lau<u>gh</u>
g	<u>g</u>irl, di<u>g</u>
h	<u>h</u>ip
j	<u>j</u>ump, gru<u>dge</u>
k	<u>c</u>at, ta<u>ck</u>
l	<u>l</u>ie, pi<u>ll</u>
m	<u>m</u>an, na<u>m</u>e
n	<u>n</u>ail, ca<u>n</u>
ng	ri<u>ng</u>, ha<u>ng</u>er
p	<u>p</u>it, ti<u>p</u>
r	<u>r</u>ed, bu<u>r</u>
s	<u>s</u>at, pa<u>ss</u>
sh	<u>sh</u>ip, di<u>sh</u>
t	<u>t</u>op, po<u>t</u>
th	<u>th</u>in, ba<u>th</u>
w	<u>w</u>ill, fe<u>w</u>
y	<u>y</u>ell, can<u>y</u>on
z	<u>z</u>ip, car<u>s</u>
zh	bei<u>g</u>e, mea<u>s</u>ure

absit omen *ahb-sit oh-men*\

(Latin) "May this not be an omen." This is used when something foreboding happens. It is a plea for divine protection against the terrible thing you fear is to come.

academia *a-ku-dee-mee-yah*\

(Latin) The educational environment and the culture of the university. From *academia* comes the slang term "academese" for impenetrable jargon written by academics.

a cappella *ah kah-pe-lah*\

(Italian) Singing without instrumental accompaniment.

achtung *ahk-toong*\

(German) Look out! Danger.

actus dei *ahk-toos dey-ee*\

(Latin) "Act of God." Used in legal terminology because everything sounds more official in Latin.

ad astra per aspera *ad as-trah per as-pe-rah*\

(Latin) "To the stars through difficulties." The state motto of Kansas.

addendum \u-dend-um\
(Latin) An extra item added at the end of a publication or book.

ad hoc \ad hok\
(Latin) "To this." Created for a particular purpose; often attached to the word "committee."

adieu \ah-dyoo\
(French) *Adieu* is what you say when you do not expect to see someone again: "good-bye forever." The everyday way of saying "good-bye" in French is *au revoir*, which means "until we see each other again."

ad libitum \ad lib-i-tum\
(Latin) At one's pleasure, extemporaneously. We generally shorten this to "ad lib."

ad nauseum \ad nau-zee-yum\
(Latin) "To sickness." Something that has been done to death. "He went on about his stamp collection *ad nauseum*."

advocatus diaboli
\ad-voh-kah-toos dee-ah-boh-lee\
(Latin) "The devil's advocate."

affaire de coeur \a-fer de ker\
(French) A love affair.

aficionado \a-fish-ee-oh-nah-doh\
(Spanish) An enthusiastic amateur. "He is an *aficionado* of Elvis impersonators." (See page 63.)

a fortiori \ey for-shee-or-eye\
(Latin) "With even stronger reason." It refers to an inference that if a first thing is true, the second proposition must be even more true. "I don't trust him to balance his checkbook, so *a fortiori* I do not trust him to run a company."

agape \ah-gah-pey\
(Greek) Selfless Christian fraternal love.

agar \a-gar\
(Malay) Also known as *agar-agar*, a jelly made from seaweed. It is used as an ingredient in desserts, as a vegetarian substitute for gelatin, and as a basic ingredient of bacterial culture media.

agent provocateur \a-zhahn pro-vo-kah-ter\
(French) A person who tries to draw another into a crime or misdeed.

ahisma \ah-heez-mah\
(Sanskrit) A spirit of compassion and nonviolence.

aide-de-camp \eyd de kamp\

(French) The assistant of a military officer. It is sometimes applied in a political context for anyone who acts on behalf of a more senior person.

aikido \eye-kee-doh\

(Japanese) A Japanese martial art whose name literally means "method of adapting to the spirit."

akita \ah-kee-tah\

(Japanese) A breed of dog of the spitz family.

à la carte \ah lah kahrt\

(French) "From the menu." A restaurant meal in which items are priced individually. (See also *prix fixe*.)

à la minute \ah lah mee-noot\

(French) "In the minute." This is culinary-speak for a dish that is made to order instead of being prepared in a big batch in advance.

à la mode \ah la mohd\

(French) Literally this means "in fashion," but in the United States, it is more frequently used to mean "topped with ice cream."

al dente \al den-tey\
(Italian) "To the teeth." When cooking pasta, it means to take the noodles out of the water while they are a bit firm.

alfresco \al-fres-koh\
(Italian) In the open air. Outside.

algor mortis \al-gor mor-tis\
(Latin) The cooling of a body following death.

alias \ey-lee-us\
(Latin) An assumed name.

alibi \al-i-beye\
(Latin) A piece of evidence that accounts for one's whereabouts at the time a crime was committed.

Allahu Akbar \ah-lah-hoo ahk-bahr\
(Arabic) "God is great." It is spoken at the beginning of the Muslim prayer cycle.

allegro \a-leg-roh\
(Italian) Music played at a brisk pace.

alma mater \ahl-mah mah-ter\
(Latin) "Bountiful mother." First used metaphorically in 1710 to refer to one's university or school and the usage stuck.

alpha \al-fah\
(Greek) *Alpha* is the first letter of the Greek alphabet and is metaphorically applied to anything that comes first; for example, an "alpha male."

alter ego \ahl-tur ee-goh\
(Latin) An alternative persona. Superman is Clark Kent's *alter ego*.

NOT THAT KIND OF LARK
ALOUETTE \a-loo-et\

An *alouette* is a "lark"—as in the bird, not a merry and frolicking escapade—and the song by this name comes to us from French Canadian fur trappers who presumably sang it whilst cleaning the bird after a good day's hunting. "Lark, nice lark, I pluck you," the song says. In everyday French the final "e" is not voiced, but it is traditional to pronounce the "e" at the end of a word in poetry and song \a-loo-eh-tuh\.

amanuensis *ah-mahn-yoo-en-sis*\

(Latin) This high-falutin' term for a literary or artistic assistant may not be complimentary, as it translates to "a slave at hand."

ambiance *ahm-bee-ahns*\

(French) The atmosphere or mood of a place.

âme damnée *ahm dahm-ney*\

(French) A "lost soul" who mindlessly follows someone undeserving. A dupe.

amicus curiae *a-mi-kus kyoor-ee-ey*\

(Latin) "A friend of the court." Someone who is not a party to the litigation but is invited to give advice on the matter.

amigo *u-mee-goh*\

(Spanish) "Friend."

amok *ah-muk*\

(Portugese, from Malay) The way a frenzied person runs. Have you ever heard *amok* when it was not paired with "run"? (See page 192.)

amor fati *ah-mor fah-tee*\

(Latin) "Love of fate." Loving all of life, including its joys and its sorrows and pains.

amour propre \ah-moor pro-pr\
(French) Proper love is self-love. It refers to a sense of self-worth, self-confidence.

amuse-bouche \ah-mooz boosh\
(French) Something to "amuse the mouth." A small appetizer.

anathema \a-na-the-ma\
(Latin) Borrowed from ecclesiastical Latin, which borrowed the term from the Greek, it was originally a votive offering but evolved to mean an excommunicated person or anything accursed or damned. Most often it is now used in an entirely secular context to indicate something the speaker dislikes.

angst \angst\
(German) In English angst is a particularly deep form of dread or anxiety. It is the everyday word Germans use for "worry."

anima mundi \a-nee-mah mun-dee\
(Latin) "The soul of the world." It refers to the concept that the world is a living being with its own spirit, and that all of the living things on the planet are connected to this organism.

anime \a-ni-mey\
(Japanese) Americans use the general Japanese word for "animation" to refer to a specific style of Japanese animation that often has adult themes.

SALUTATIONS!

There are as many ways to say "hello" and "good-bye" as there are languages, and English has done a good job of appropriating a lot of these pleasantries. But what are the actual translations of these *guten Tag*s and *aloha*s?

In France, they say *bonjour*, which translates to "good" (*bon*) "day" (*jour*). You can also say "good evening" with *bonne soir* or "good night" with *bonne nuit*.

The Germans will give you a *guten Morgen* to wish you good morning, a *guten Abend* in the afternoon, and a *guten Tag* any old time of day.

In Hawaii, *aloha* can be used for "hello" or "good-bye," and even though it doesn't translate to "good" as with common French and German greetings, it can be used in much the same way. You can say *aloha kakahiaka* for "good morning," *aloha auinala* for "good afternoon," and *aloha ahiahi* for "good evening." Its literal meaning, however, comes from *alo*, meaning "presence" or "face," and *ha*, which means "breath." The combined term is "the presence of breath," and the deeper meaning is the way of living in which you love and respect others as well as yourself.

In Arabic, people greet each other *salaam alaikum*, which means "peace upon you." Like *aloha*, it has a deeper spiritual connotation than a "good day" greeting and it can be used upon meeting or parting with someone. The typical response is *wa-alaikum-salaam*, "and upon you peace."

In Spanish, you can wish someone a "good day" by saying *buenos días*, or a "good afternoon" with *buenas tardes*, and "good evening" with *buenas noches*, but this last phrase is only used as a greeting and not as a parting.

The Italians say *ciao* for both "hello" and "good-bye," but you really shouldn't throw this salutation around unless you actually know the person. It comes from the phrase *s-ciào vostro* of the Venetian dialect, which translates to "I am your slave." It was not a salutation that was used literally, but rather as a pleasantry like "I am at your service" or "if you need something, let me know." Still, it has a very familiar air to it.

ankh *ahnk*\\
(Egyptian) A symbol of life consisting of a cross topped by a loop.

anno domini *ah-no do-min-ee*\\
(Latin) Abbreviated AD, it means "in the year of the Lord." A reference to the birth year of Jesus of Nazareth. (Although, scholars now believe Jesus was actually born between the years 7 and 4 BCE, not in 1 AD.)

annuit coeptis *an-yoo-it koip-tees*\\
(Latin) "God has favored our undertaking." Appears on the back of the great seal of the United States.

annus horribilis *ah-nus hor-i-bi-lus*\\
(Latin) "A terrible year."

anorak *a-nor-ak*\\
(Danish) A weatherproof jacket.

anschluss *ahn-shloos*\\
(German) Also spelled *Anschluß*. It means "to join" and it refers to the annexation of Austria by Germany in 1938.

antediluvian *an-tee-di-loo-vee-en*\\
(Latin) Before the deluge, referring to Noah's flood. More

broadly, it is used to describe a time before a catastrophic event, or simply a very long time ago.

apartheid \ah-par-tayt\
(Afrikaans) "Apartness." Refers to the official government policy of racial segregation in South Africa, abolished in the 1990s. It is sometimes applied to any system which segregates people by race or social class.

aperitif \ah-per-i-teef\
(French) Wine or liquor taken before a meal to stimulate one's appetite.

apnea \ap-nee-ah\
(Greek) A temporary stoppage of breathing during sleep.

apocrypha \a pok-ri-fah\
(Greek) "Things hidden away." Usually used in reference to ancient religious texts which were used as scripture by various early Christian groups but excluded from the official canon of the Bible. The Roman Catholic Church, the Eastern Orthodox Church, and the Protestant Church have slightly differing views on which books are canonical and which are *apocryphal*.

à point \ah pwahn\
(French) In culinary terminology, this means to cook to the ideal state of doneness.

apologia \a-pol-oh-jee-ah\
(Latin) Not an apology, but a written defense of one's position.

après moi, le déluge \ah-prey mwah le dey-loozh\
(French) "After me, the flood." The Marquise de Pompadour said this to Louis XV after the defeat of the French army in the battle of Rossbach. It is used when someone acts irresponsibly, unconcerned about the long-term consequences. "Global warming? Whatever. I like my Hummer. *Après moi, le déluge.*"

a priori \ah pree-oh-ree\
(Latin) Knowledge gained independent of experience. "We intuit the existence of a higher being *a priori.*" —Immanuel Kant

apropos \a-pro-poh\
(French) "By the way" or "on that subject."

aqua vitae \ak-wah vee-tay\
(Latin) Although it means "water of life," the phrase refers to strong liquor.

arabesque \a-ra-besk\
(French) "In the style of the Arabs." It is used in various contexts in the arts. For example, it is used to refer to a particular form of decorative Islamic art. In ballet it is a pose with the body bent forward and the back leg extended. (Do Arabs do that?)

argot *ahr-goh*\\

(French) *Argot* means "slang" in French, but it came to be associated specifically with the inside jargon of con artists and thieves.

argumentum ad hominem
   ahr-gyoo-ment-um ahd hom-in-um\\

(Latin) Attacking the character of a person rather than the substance of his argument. Also called an *"ad hominem* attack."

armamentarium *ahr-mah-men-ta-ree-um*\\

(Latin) "An arsenal" or "armory." In medicine it refers to the assortment of remedies available to combat a disease or injury.

arpeggio *ahr-pe-jee-oh*\\

(Italian) The notes of a chord played in rapid succession rather than all at once.

arrivederci *a-ree-vah-der-chee*\\

(Italian) Good-bye, until we meet again.

ars gratia artis *ahrz graht-ee-ah ahr-tis*\\

(Latin) "Art for art's sake." The motto of MGM appearing at the beginning of films in the logo that encircles the roaring lion.

artiste \ahr-teest\
(French) *Artiste* is simply the French word for "artist." But when it is pronounced in the French manner, it implies the person in question has pretensions to seriousness that may not be warranted.

ashram \ash-rahm\
(Sanskrit) A Hindu monastic community.

au contraire \oh con-trer\
(French) A fancy French way of saying "on the contrary."

au courant \oh coo-rahn\
(French) Up to date, aware of the latest goings-on.

auf wiedersehen \awf vee-der-seyn\
(German) Good-bye. (If you're a contestant on *Project Runway*, it means you're not going to Fashion Week.)

au gratin \oh grah-tan\
(French) Cooked with a brown, crusted top, usually of cheese.

au jus \oh zhoo\
(French) "With juice." In the language of the kitchen, it means meat roasted in its natural juices.

auld lang syne *ahld lang zeyen*\\
(Scottish Gaelic) Literally "old long since" or, in better English, "days gone by."

au naturel *oh na-tur-el*\\
(French) "As in nature." Naked.

aurora australis *ah-ror-ah ah-stral-is*\\
(Latin) The southern lights.

aurora borealis *ah-ror-ah bor-ee-al-is*\\
(Latin) The northern lights.

auteur *oh-toor*\\
(French) "Author." In cinema parlance, it refers to a director who has complete artistic control over his *oeuvre*.

autobahn *oh-toh-bahn*\\
(German) The German word for "highway." Used when talking about freeways in German-speaking countries.

auto-da-fé *oh-toh dah fey*\\
(Portuguese) Literally "act of faith," the expression was used for the ceremony surrounding the pronouncement of judgments by the Spanish Inqusition and thus came to mean the burning of a heretic.

avant-garde \ah-vahn gard\
(French) Edgy, experimental art.

ave \ah-vey\
(Latin) *Ave* means "hail." Thus *Ave Maria* means "Hail Maria."

avtomat Kalashnikov \av-toh-mat kal-ash-ni-kov\
(Russian) This is the full version of the abbreviation AK, as in the AK-47 rifle. Mikhail Kalashnikov was its inventor.

ayatollah \ay-ah-tol-ah\
(Persian) The leader of the Iranian Muslim Shiite religion.

ay caramba \ay kah-rahm-bah\
(Spanish) *Caramba* is a mild obscenity derived from a euphemism for the male member. An exclamation of surprise similar in force to "darn it." It's also a catchphrase of the cartoon character Bart Simpson.

ayurveda \ay-ur-ve-dah\
(Sanskrit) Traditional Hindu system of medicine.

babu *bah-boo*\

(Hindi) Used as a courtesy title for Hindu gentlemen. In the U.K., it is sometimes used as a slur toward Indian immigrants who are not fully fluent in English.

babushka *ba-bush-kah*\

(Russian) Literally, it means "grandmother," but it can be applied to any old lady and also to the type of headscarf an old lady might wear.

baccalaureate *bak-ah-lor-ee-at*\

(Latin) A university degree.

bagatelle *bag-ah-tel*\

(French) A short piece of music in a light style.

bain-marie *bahn mah-ree*\

(French) In cooking and chemistry, a *bain marie* is a large pan filled with hot water in which another smaller pan can be placed to maintain a steady temperature or to cook something slowly. This, in literal French, is a "bath of Mary." It seems this is because mother Mary bathes you in a gentle warmth, like the pan.

balalaika \bal-ah-layk-ah\

(Russian) A musical instrument that looks like a small, triangular guitar.

bambino \bam-bee-no\

(Italian) A baby or young child.

banya \bahn-yah\

(Russian) A Russian steamroom.

banzai \ban-zay\

(Japanese) An interjection shouted as a battle cry or an expression of enthusiasm. (Not to be confused with *bonsai*, an ornamental, miniature tree.)

bar mitzvah \bar mits-vah\

(Hebrew) In popular parlance, a Jewish coming-of-age celebration held when a boy turns thirteen. Traditionally, a boy *becomes bar mitzvah*, a "son of the commandment," at thirteen, when he gains the status and the responsibility of an adult under Jewish law. (See also *bat mitzvah* and *mitzvah*.)

barre \bar\

(French) *Barre* is pronounced "bar" and means "bar." Ballet dancers use the French word for what they grasp to exercise because the ballet world is like that.

barrio *bah-ree-yoh*\
(Spanish) A densely populated urban area where Spanish-speaking people live.

basso profundo *bas-oh pro-foon-doh*\
(Italian) A singer with very low vocal range; a deep bass.

basta *bahs-tah*\
(Italian) "Enough!" Used in exasperation.

batik *bah-teek*\
(Javanese) This Javanese word for "painted" is applied to a specific method of coloring textiles.

bat mitzvah *baht mits-vah*\
(Hebrew) The female equivalent of the *bar mitzvah*, attained when a girl turns twelve. Ceremonies to mark the occasion are not traditional and did not become common until the middle of the twentieth century. (See also *bar mitzvah* and *mitzvah*.)

bazaar *bah-zahr*\
(Persian) A large public market. (A strange public market would be a "bizarre bazaar.")

beaucoup *boh-koo*\
(French) "Lots of." It is gaining currency in American slang, as in "He has *beaucoup* bucks."

Mock Italian

BRAGGADOCIO

This word for pompous boasting certainly sounds Italian, but it was coined as a character name in 1590 by Edmund Spenser in *Faerie Queene*. Braggadocio was a boastful coward. Spenser came up with the name by fusing the word "braggart" (which, incidentally, has a French root) with an Italian-sounding suffix "occio."

Similarly, Paparazzi (plural for *paparazzo*) was a fictional character. The photographer character appeared in the 1959 Fellini film *La Dolce Vita*. The name had no particular significance before that.

Svengali, a person who exerts mental control over another, was a character in George du Maurier's 1894 novel *Trilby*.

beau sabreur *boh sa-brur*\

(French) "A handsome swordsman." A dashing, heroic man. Prince Charming.

beaux arts *bohz ahr*\

(French) Fine arts, and also more specifically, a particular school of decorative arts in nineteenth-century France.

bel canto *bel kan-toh*\

(Italian) "Fine song." A style of operatic singing.

bel esprit *bel es-pree*\

(French) A person who has wit, charm, and social graces.

belle époque *bel ey-pok*\

(French) A period of comfort and prosperity.

belle laide *bel led*\

(French) "Beautiful-ugly." It refers to a woman who is attractive but not conventionally beautiful.

bento *ben-toh*\

(Japanese) A meal served in a box that is divided into sections.

bête noire *bet noo-wahr*\

(French) Literally, a "black beast," figuratively, something strongly disliked.

bidet \bee-dey\
(French) A small basin, similar to a toilet, used, in the immortal words of Crocodile Dundee, "to wash your backside."

bijou \bee-zhoo\
(French) "A jewel." The plural is *bijoux* and is pronounced the same as in the singular. French is like that.

bildungsroman \bil-dungz-roh-man\
(German) A coming-of-age novel.

billabong \bi-le-bong\
(Indigenous Australian) A branch of a river that forms a stagnant pool when water flows from the main stream during a flood. Used primarily in the singing of "Waltzing Matilda."

billet doux \bee-yey doo\
(French) A love letter.

bishonen \bee-show-nen\
(Japanese) "Beautiful boy." Refers to a particular type of androgynous, pretty, young man, a fixture in Japanese pop culture. The word is popular among *anime* and *manga* fans.

bivouac \biv-oo-wak\
(French) A temporary camp without tents.

blasé \blah-zey\
(French) Unimpressed, with a touch of "been there, done that."

bleu de France \ble de frahns\
(French) A bright shade of blue.

blitzkrieg \blits-kreeg\
(German) "Lightning war." A swift and decisive military attack.
Shock and awe. Mostly used in reference to World War II.

bodega \boh dey-gah\
(Spanish) A small grocery store, usually in a Spanish-
speaking area.

bodhisattva \boh-dee-saht-vah\
(Sanskrit) An enlightened being who refrains from entering
nirvana in order to assist other beings in obtaining
enlightenment.

bolero \boh-ler-oh\
(Spanish) This word refers both to a Spanish dance and to a
short jacket that reaches just to the waist.

Bolshevik \bol-she-vik\
(Russian) A member of the Communist party, specifically, the
Social Democratic Party, which seized control of Russia in
1917. By extension, any socialist or lefty.

bona fide *boh-nah feyed*\
(Latin) Confirmed genuine or "in good faith." "He made a *bona fide* attempt to deliver the *bona fide* article."

bon appétit *bon a-pe-teet*\
(French) It means "good appetite" and people say this to indicate that it is time to start eating.

bongo *bon-goh*\
(Spanish) Bongo drums originated in Cuba and are the principal drums for a number of forms of Afro-Caribbean music.

bonhomie *bah-nah-mee*\
(French) A positive, friendly nature.

bon mot *bon moh*\
(French) "Good word." A well-turned phrase; usually a witty one.

bon vivant *bon vi-vahnt*\
(French) A person who takes pleasure in life.

bon voyage *bon voy-ahzh*\
(French) Used to wish someone well before a journey.

boomerang *boom-er-ang*\
(Indigenous Australian) A bent piece of wood that is designed to come back when you throw it (but usually doesn't).

FRENCH VS. YIDDISH
BOLDNESS

PANACHE

The word *panache* first appeared in English in a translation of Edmond Rostand's *Cyrano de Bergerac*. (If you just use the French word because you can't think of an English equivalent does that really count as "translation"?) Like Cyrano, this French word for confidence and boldness has more than a small dose of theatricality. You have *panache* if you command your space in a particularly stylish way.

CHUTZPAH

The Yiddish *chutzpah* is more defiant than its French counterpart. *Panache* would try to charm its boss into giving it a raise. *Chutzpah* would march into the office and announce it was now earning an additional four thousand dollars a year.

THE WINNER?

Yiddish. Bet on *chutzpah* to whip *panache* in a fight, but *panache* might just persuade you that losing was all part of its plan. *En garde!*

borracho \boh-rah-choh\
(Spanish) Drunk. (If you can still roll the *R*s, you are probably not that *borracho* yet.)

boudoir \boo-dwahr\
(French) A woman's bedroom, the place where she does her makeup and personal grooming.

bouquet \boo-key\
(French) An assemblage of pretty flowers.

bouquet garni \boo-key gahr-nee\
(French) A cheesecloth bundle of fresh herbs and vegetables used to flavor soup or sauce.

bourgeois \boor-zhwah\
(French) Middle class and conventional.

bravo \brah-voh\
(French) *Aficionados* of classical arts shout this to indicate that they are educated enough to appreciate a fine performance and cheer for it in French.

bravura \brah-voo-rah\
(Italian) Brilliant technical skill. The term has a sense of high energy. It is often used to describe solos by male dancers.

brogan *bro-gan*\
(Gaelic) A leather shoe that reaches to the ankle.

bubbe *bu-bey* or *bu-bee*\
(Yiddish) Grandmother, or an old lady who calls to mind a grandmother.

bupkes or **bupkis** *bup-kes*\
(Yiddish) It literally means "goat or sheep excrement." Figuratively, it means something about as valuable as goat pellets. "I worked all day, and what do I have to show for it? *Bupkes.*"

bürgermeister *bur-gur meye-stur*\
(German) "Master of the people who live in the town." Mayor. The 1970 Rankin-Bass Christmas special *Santa Claus Is Comin' to Town* famously featured a baddy called "Bürgermeister Meisterburger."

burka *bur-ke*\
(Urdu) A long garment covering both the body and face with a mesh to see through, worn by Muslim women in public in some Middle Eastern nations.

burro *bur-roh*\
(Spanish) A donkey.

cadaver \ka-da-ver\
(Latin) A dead body. (See page 47.)

caduceus \kah-doo-see-yus\
(Latin) A staff with two serpents coiled around it, the symbol of the medical profession.

canard \ka-nar\
(French) Literally, *canard* is the French word for "duck." We use *canard* to mean a "hoax," because back when more English people spoke French, we used the full expression *vendre un canard à moitié*—that is, "to half-sell a duck," i.e., to cheat.

candombe \kan-dom-bey\
(Spanish) A rhythmic musical style brought to Uruguay by African slaves.

capo di tutti capi \ka-poh dee too-tee ka-pee\
(Italian) The boss of bosses. Usually used in reference to the Italian mafia.

capotasto *ka-poh-tas-toh*\\
(Italian) Usually shortened to *capo* *key-poh*\\, a steel bar that changes the tuning of a guitar when clamped along the fingerboard.

carpe diem *kar-pey dee-yem*\\
(Latin) "Seize the day." It dates back to a poem by Horace, but it was popularized in nonscholarly circles by Robin Williams' character in the movie *Dead Poets Society*.

carte blanche *kart blahnsh*\\
(French) Permission to do whatever one likes. Originally, a blank paper signed by one person and given to another, allowing the second person to write in his own conditions. A blank check.

carte de visite *kart de vi-zeet*\\
(French) A small photograph mounted on a card.

castrato *ka-strah-toh*\\
(Italian) A male opera singer castrated before puberty in order to preserve the high register of his voice. There are thankfully not any of these around anymore: the last castrato, Alessandro Moreschi, died in 1922.

casus belli *ka-sus be-lee*\\
(Latin) "The cause of war." (*Belli* is also the root of the word "bellicose.")

catamaran *kat-ah-mah-ran*\\
(Tamil) A boat with two hulls.

catharsis *ka-thar-sis*\\
(Greek) Emotional cleansing. Profound relief.

CHEFS OUTSIDE THE KITCHEN

What do Bobby Flay, Barack Obama, and Sitting Bull have in common? They are all chiefs. The term we use for the head *honcho* in the kitchen comes from the modern French word *chef,* which means leader. In Old French this was the "head of a family or clan," and it came into English around 1570. This meaning was later applied to the leaders of Native American tribes. The term "Commander-in-Chief" dates back to 1660. The modern French *chef de cuisine* entered our language in 1830, and the term quickly abbreviated to its first, and now-ubiquitous, word.

cathexis \ka-thek-sis\

(Greek) This word is not widely used outside of psychoanalysis, but is useful enough that it should be. It means the concentration of mental energy on a particular person or idea, with the suggestion that it is an unhealthy obsession. "Mary Ann's *cathexis* for Bob prevented her from noticing that John was in love with her."

cause célèbre \kahs sey-leb-ru\

(French) A celebrated cause.

caveat \ka-vee-aht\

(Latin) Stipulations. Or, warning. "You have been approved to operate the nuclear submarine with a few *caveats*."

caveat emptor \ka-vee-aht emp-tor\

(Latin) "Let the buyer beware." If you buy a lemon from a slick-talking car dealer, you have only yourself to blame.

cedilla \se-dee-yu\

(Spanish) The little hook under the letter *c* in French words (ç) that indicates it is pronounced like an *s* rather than like a *k*.

ceilidh \key-lee\

(Gaelic) A Scottish or Irish social event with traditional music and dancing.

c'est la guerre *sey lah ger*\\
(French) "That's war." Meaning "stuff happens."

c'est la vie *sey lah vee*\\
(French) "That's life."

chacun à son goût *shak-un ah sun goot*\\
(French) "To each his own taste." In English, we'd say "to each his own."

chador *shah-der*\\
(Persian) A full body cloak worn in public by some Iranian women.

chaise longue *shez long*\\
(French) It's a long chair. We could call it a long chair, but instead we call it *chaise longue*, which means "long chair" in French.

chakra *shak-rah*\\
(Sanskrit) One of the body's seven centers of spiritual power.

chaud-froid *show-fwah*\\
(French) "Hot-cold." A dish that is cooked and then chilled before being served.

Latin vs. French
BRING OUT YOUR DEAD!

Cadaver
The Latin word *cadaver* derives from *cadere* "to be slain in battle." Thus, it is more often used in a medical context than the French *corpse*. The sense is that the body has been sacrificed for the greater good of educating medical students.

Corpse
The French word we've adopted for what is left behind when we have shuffled off our mortal coil is the same word they use for the body of a living person (less the final *e*, which was not commonly tacked on until the nineteenth century). Meaning "body" in the collective sense, it is used in such expressions as "Marine Corps" and *corps de ballet*.

The Winner?
Cadaver. The Romans have conquered thanks to the nuance of nobility. See also *rigor mortis*.

chauffeur *show-fer*\

(French) A professional driver. The word dates back to the days when motor cars had steam engines and had to be heated up (the French for "to heat" is *chauffer*) before they would start.

ITALIAN SPELLED BADLY

Italian words are fun to borrow. There is the musical cadence of the language and the Italian habit of broad hand gestures. When you've had enough you can shout "*Basta!*" and throw your hands up with a flourish. Another popular Italian-ism has just a hint of Mafia movie chic about it. When you want to make sure someone gets your point you can say "*Capeesh*?" This supposedly means "Do you understand?" in Italian. It comes from *capisce*, which is the third-person singular form of the verb *capire*. So when you write *capeesh*, you're spelling it wrong, and when you say it, you're really asking, "Does he understand?" (*Capite* is actually the second-person formal or plural form.)

chef de cuisine *shef de kwee-zeen*\
(French) "The leader of the kitchen." A head chef. (See page 44.)

chef d'équipe *shef dey-keep*\
(French) Team leader.

chef d'oeuvre *she doo-vru*\
(French) A masterpiece. One's primary work of art.

cher maître *sher met-re*\
(French) "Dear master." A title for a respected and loved artistic mentor.

chiaroscuro *kee-ahr-os-koo-roh*\
(Italian) A painting technique in which there is a stark contrast between light and dark.. *Chiaro* is "light" and *oscuro* is "dark." The Italian baroque painter Caravaggio was a master of this form.

chiasmus *ki-az-mus*\
(Greek) A rhetorical term in which the second clause or phrase inverts the text of the opening clause or phrase. Example: "Ask not what your country can do for you, ask what you can do for your country."

c

chic \sheek\
(French) Cool, fashionable, and elegant. (Also the name of the 1970s disco band who recorded "Le Freak.")

chicano \chi-kah-no\
(Mexican Spanish) A Mexican-Spanish term for a Mexican-American. *Chicanismo* is pride in being *chicano*.

chichi \shee-shee\
(French) Describes someone trying to be *chic* but only managing to be pretentious.

chignon \sheen-yon\
(French) A hairstyle consisting of a knot at the nape of the neck.

chimera \kay-mer-ah\
(Latin, from Greek) Originally, a mythological beast with the head of a lion, the body of a goat, and the tail of a dragon. Metaphorically, its meaning has drifted to "wild fantasy" or "illusion."

chinook \shi-nook\
(Salish) A warm, moist wind blowing from the ocean onto the coast of the Pacific Northwest. Salish or Salishan is a group of twenty-three languages once spoken by the indigenous residents of the region. All of the languages are now extinct or endangered.

chinos *chee-nohz*\\
(Spanish) Cotton trousers.

chutzpah *hoots-pah*\\
(Yiddish) Audacious boldness. (See page 39.)

ciao *chow*\\
(Italian) A salutation that can be used for "hello" and "good-bye." (See page 23.)

circa *sir-ku*\\
(Latin) Around a particular date. Abbreviated *ca*. "The student was not well informed. She thought the Battle of the Bulge took place *circa* 1968."

clave *klah-vey*\\
(Spanish) A musical rhythm used in Afro-Cuban music, such as the rumba.

cliché *klee-shey*\\
(French) From a French term from a type of printing block, also known as a "stereotype block," comes the notion of a verbal or written phrase that is nothing but an unoriginal copy.

coda *koh-dah*\\
(Italian) The final section of a piece of music or work of literature.

¡CHE!

Of course you've heard of the Argentinian Marxist revolutionary Che Guevara. (Maybe you even had a picture of him on the wall of your college dorm room.) Che *chey*\ was actually a nickname for Mr. Ernesto Guevara. So what does it mean? *Che* is a catch-all word in Argentine Spanish. You call it out when you want to get someone's attention, like "Hey!" It can be used to mean "buddy" or "mate," for example, when you can't remember someone's name. It is also the space-saver word that Argentinians use to fill a pause in conversation while their brains are catching up to their tongues. The English equivalent would be "uh" or "um." Che got his nickname from other Spanish speakers as a playful dig at his Argentine linguistic habits. So Che Guevara can be translated to "Hey You Guevara."

codex \koh-deks\
(Latin) A manuscript of an ancient text. The plural is "codices."

cogito ergo sum \koh-jee-toh er-goh soom\
(Latin) "I think, therefore I am." The central principle of René
Descartes' philosophy.

cognoscenti \kon-yoh-shen-tee\
(Italian) People with inside knowledge in a particular field,
usually the arts.

cojones \koh-hoh-nez\
(Spanish) The testicles, and all the courage that possessing
them metaphorically implies.

collegium \kah-lee-jee-um\
(Latin) A group united by common pursuits.

colonette \kol-oh-net\
(French) A small column, such as one used to hold up a porch.

colossus \ko-los-us\
(Latin) A giant thing.

comme ci, comme ça \kum see kum sah\
(French) "Like this, like that." Neither good nor bad. It can be
used with a shrug to answer "How's it going?" with "Eh."

comme il faut \kum eel foh\
(French) Proper, conforming to accepted standards.

compadre \kom-pah-drey\
(Spanish) *Compadre* originally meant "godfather," but it has evolved to mean a companion or friend.

compos mentis \kom-pos men-tis\
(Latin) Used in the legal arena to mean having full control of one's mental faculties.

MOCK CHINESE
CHOW CHOW

Unlike the *Shar Pei* and the *Shih Tzu* dog breeds, which take their names from Cantonese and Mandarin respectively, *Chow Chow* is named in *faux* Chinese. It is how Western ears interpreted the Mandarin *Songshi Quan*, a lovely, descriptive name that means "puffy lion dog."

concierge *kon-see-erzh*\
(French) A porter or doorkeeper of a hotel or apartment.

connoisseur *kon-i-soo-er*\
(French) Someone who is knowledgeable in something. And possibly snobby about it as well.

conquistador *kon-kees-tah-dor*\
(Spanish) Originally, the Spanish conquerors of Latin America; more broadly, anyone who conquers.

consigliere *kon-seel-yer-e*\
(Italian) An advisor, especially to a crime boss.

continuum *kon-tin-yoo-um*\
(Latin) An unbroken series or progression. "While many believe people are either gay or straight, Kinsey thought sexual orientation was a *continuum*."

contra bonos mores *kon-trah boh-nos moh-reys*\
(Latin) A legal term referring to behavior that is harmful to the moral welfare of society. "This contract to have Justin Bieber perform a concert at the Anne Frank House is *contra bonos mores* and is therefore null and void."

C

contralto _kon-tral-toh_\\

(Italian) A singer with a range that falls below soprano and above tenor.

contretemps _kon-tre-tem_\\

(French) A humiliating moment, unfortunate event, or argument.

coolibah _koo-li-bah_\\

(Yuwaaliyaay, Indigenous Australian) The word is best known for its inclusion in the song "Waltzing Matilda." It is a type of eucalyptus tree.

coquette _koh-ket_\\

(French) A flirtatious woman. English has adopted an adjectival form, "coquettish."

cordon bleu _kor-don ble_\\

(French) "Blue ribbon." The term referred to award-winning chefs and their signature dishes. More often these days, it appears on menus to refer to a particular dish rolled up and filled with cheese and ham, whether award-winning or not.

corps de ballet _kor de ba-ley_\\

(French) "The body of the ballet." The group of dancers who perform the large synchronized pieces or provide the background in classical ballet performances.

corpus delicti \\kor-pus de-lik-teye\\
(Latin) "The body of the offense," or the circumstances that make up a crime.

corrida \\kor-ee-dah\\
(Spanish) From the word for "race" comes *corrida de toros*, the "running of the bulls," and *corrida* for "bullfight."

Cosa Nostra \\koh-sah noh-strah\\
(Italian) *Cosa Nostra* means "our thing," where "thing" means organized crime.

coup de foudre \\koo de foo-dre\\
(French) Literally it is a "bolt of lightning," but metaphorically it is love at first sight.

coup de grâce \\koo de grahs\\
(French) The death blow.

coup d'état \\koo dey-tah\\
(French) A sudden overthrow of power.

coup de théâtre \\koo de tey-ah-tre\\
(French) "A stroke of theater." A dramatic turn of events. It can be used literally in reference to a theatrical performance or more metaphorically for a stagey and surprising act in life.

credo \kree-doh\
(Latin) "I believe." A statement of personal belief.

credo quia absurdum est
  \kree-doh kwee-ah ahb-soor-dum est\
(Latin) "I believe it because it is unreasonable." An appeal to
faith rather than logic.

crème de la crème \krem de lah krem\
(French) The cream of the cream, the top of the top, the
cat's meow.

cri de coeur \kree de kur\
(French) An emotional appeal, a "cry of the heart."

croupier \kroop-ee-ey\
(French) An attendant at a gambling table who rakes in chips
and pays the winners. (But more often rakes in the chips.)

(la) cucaracha \koo-ka-rah-chah\
(Spanish) "Cockroach." The word is widely known thanks to
a popular Mexican folk song about an insect who can't travel
because it doesn't have any *marijuana* to smoke.

cuisine \kwee-zeen\

(French) "The kitchen." (A *chef de cuisine* is the chief of the kitchen.) It can be used more generally to refer to cooking and dining. (See pages 44 and 49.)

cul de sac \kul de sak\

(French) A *cul de sac* is the bottom of a sac, or bag, which kind of resembles a road that ends in a circle when you think about it.

cum laude \koom low-du\

(Latin) This academic title translates to "with honor." It is slightly less "honorable" than *magna cum laude* and *summa cum laude*.

czar \zahr\

(Russian) Also spelled (and sometimes pronounced) *tsar*. A title meaning "emperor," derived from the name of the Roman emperor Caesar. By extension, any person who is in charge of an organization, especially used in politics. "We need to appoint an energy *czar*."

da capo \dah kah-poh\
(Italian) A musical instruction to repeat a phrase from the beginning.

dacha \dah-chah\
(Russian) A Russian city-dweller's small vacation cottage in the country.

dachshund \dok-soond\
(German) The name of the breed translates to "badger hound" because they were originally bred to hunt badgers.

Dalai Lama \dah-ley lah-mah\
(Mongolian) A *lama* is a Buddhist priest. *Dalai Lama* is a title given to the spiritual leader of Tibetan Buddhism. It literally translates to "the Ocean Lama."

damnosa hereditas \dam-no-sah her-e-dee-tahs\
(Latin) A tradition or inheritance that is more of a curse than a blessing.

danse macabre \dans mah-kah-bre\
(French) Dance of death.

danseur noble *dans-er no-ble*\\

(French) A term largely used by dance critics for a leading male principal dancer. There is no masculine equivalent for the word "ballerina." Male dancers are usually referred to as "dancer."

debacle *de-bah-kul*\\

(French) A complete disaster caused by failure. A catastrophic mistake.

déclassé *dey-klah-sey*\\

(French) A person or thing that has fallen in social status.

décolletage *dey-koh-le-tahzh*\\

(French) A plunging neckline, or what is revealed by one.

de facto *de fak-to*\\

(Latin) In fact, whether officially or not. Sometimes used to mean "by default." "We don't have a chairperson of that committee at the moment but Carla has been acting as the *de facto* leader."

déjà vu *dey-zhah voo*\\

(French) The sense that you have experienced this exact same moment before.

déjà vu \dey-zhah voo\
(French) The sense that you have experienced this exact same moment before.

de jure \de joor-ee\
(Latin) By legal or official right; in contrast with *de facto*.

delirium tremens \de-leer-ee-yum trem-enz\
(Latin) Uncontrollable trembling caused by alcohol withdrawal after a long period of abuse. Also known as "the d.t.s."

demi-vierge \dem-ee vee-erzh\
(French) "Half virgin." A tease or "technical virgin."

dénouement \dey-noo-mahn\
(French) The final resolution of a plot in a novel or drama.

deoch an doris \dok an doh-ris\
(Scots Gaelic) "One for the road." A last drink before you go.

deo gratiam habeamus
   \dey-oh grat-ee-ahm ha-bey-ah-mus\
(Latin) "Let us be grateful to God." The state motto of Kentucky.

Italian vs. Spanish
ENTHUSIASTIC NON-PROS

AFICIONADO

The Spanish equivalent of the French *amateur*. A person who enjoys an art (*aficionado* is often applied to bull fighting) but who doesn't do it professionally.

DILETTANTE

The Italian word for a nonprofessional artist is drawn from the verb meaning "to delight."

THE WINNER?

Although both words in their native languages refer to the joy of knowledge or creation for its own sake, *dilettante* has taken on a negative connotation in English. *Aficionado* has an assertive air of knowledge about it, perhaps because of its connection to a dangerous sport. An *aficionado* can tell you everything you need to know about his area of enjoyment. But *dilettante*, on the other hand, is a word that is often thrown at someone who thinks he or she has a real talent but is really just playing around. The Spanish are the winners of this round.

dépaysement \dey-pey-eez-mon\
(French) The feeling of disorientation that comes with being away from one's own country. The one-word version of: "Toto, I don't think we're in Kansas anymore."

de profundis \de proh-foon-dis\
(Latin) "From the depths." Perhaps best known in English as the title of Oscar Wilde's prison manuscript. The title was not assigned to it by Wilde but by his literary executor after the playwright's death. It is a reference to Psalm 130.

de rigueur \dey ri-gur\
(French) Required by custom.

dernier cri \der-nee-yer kree\
(French) "The last cry." The most up-to-date fashion.

derrière \de-ree-air\
Badonkadonk, posterior, can, rump, booty, and so on (i.e., the buttocks).

dervish \der-vish\
(Turkish) A member of an aesthetic Sufi religious order bound by vows of poverty. What made them remarkable to outsiders was a form of spinning meditation. By extension, the term "whirling dervish" is used for anyone who races about, metaphorically whirling and spinning.

desideratum \de-zid-er-ah-tum\
(Latin) Something desired; something lacking and longed for.
The plural is *desiderata*.

desuetude \des-oo-e-tood\
(French) In a state of disuse. Usually combined with the words
"fallen into."

détente \dey-tahnt\
(French) An easing of tense (diplomatic) relations.

deus ex machina \dey-oos eks mah-ki-nah\
(Latin) "God from the machine." In classical theater, dramatic
problems were sometimes solved by having a god lowered
onto the stage by a crane. This facile solution is extended
metaphorically to mean any surprising intervention that
immediately solves a complex problem as if by magic.

dharma \dahr-mu\
(Sanskrit) *Dharma* is one's sacred duty and purpose in life. It
refers to both the moral principle that shapes the universe and
a human's role in it. (See page 121.)

dharna \dahr-nu\
(Hindi) A hunger strike, sitting at the door of the person from
whom the sitter seeks a redress of grievances. (Not to be
confused with *dharma*.)

D

diaphoresis *deye-e-for-ee-sis*\\
(Greek) A pompous, medical way of saying "sweating."

didgeridoo *di-jah-ree-doo*\\
(Yolngu, an indigenous language of Northern Australia)
A distinctive growling musical instrument made out of a
hollowed-out wooden tube.

diem perdidi *dee-yem per-dee-dee*\\
(Latin) Another day wasted.

dieu et mon droit *dyoo ey mon dwah*\\
(French) "God and my right." The British monarchy's motto.

dilettante *dil-e-tahnt*\\
(Italian) An amateur dabbler. (See page 63.)

dinero *di-ne-roh*\\
(Spanish) Money.

ding an sich *ding ahn zik*\\
(German) "The thing itself." It refers to the essential quality, the
such-ness of an object before it is interpreted by the senses.

dingo *din-goh*\\
(Dharug, an extinct, indigenous Australian language) A wild
Australian dog.

dirigo \dir-ee-goh\
(Latin) "I lead." The state motto of Maine.

dirndl \dern-dul\
(German) A dress with a full peasant skirt gathered to a
tight bodice.

ditat deus \di-taht dey-oos\
(Latin) "God enriches." The state motto of Arizona.

diva \dee-vah\
(Italian) A female opera singer, or a woman who is as
spoiled as one.

divertissement \dee-ver-tees-mon\
(French) "A diversion." A short ballet between the acts of a
play or a segment in a full-length story ballet that momentarily
drops the plot, for example, to show off a series of impressive
ethnic dances for no particular narrative reason.

Doberman pinscher \doh-ber-mahn pin-cher\
(German) Doberman is a proper name, belonging to a
breeder named Ludwig Dobermann. *Pinscher* means "terrier."

dojo \doh-joh\
(Japanese) The room where people practice martial arts.

D

FALSE FRIENDS
DOUCHE \doosh\

The word we use for a solution to clean out the feminine body cavity was borrowed from the French, but on the continent, it simply means "a shower." A "gentle shower" in French, incidentally, is *une douche douce*. In America, however, it's taken on an entirely new life that has zero to do with being clean.

dolce vita \dol-chey vee-tah\
(Italian) "The sweet life." The kind of luxurious life that would appeal to a *bon vivant*.

dolchstosslegende \dol-shos-le-gen-de\
(German) "The back-stab myth." The theory cooked up by far-right-wing Germans in the aftermath of World War I to explain the nation's defeat, which claimed Jewish-Bolshevik traitors had worked behind the scenes to sabotage the war effort. By extension, it is sometimes used to refer to any similar effort to unfairly assign blame to a group the blamer already dislikes.

doloroso *doh-loh-roh-soh*\\
(Italian) A description of music played in a melancholy or sad manner.

dona nobis pacem *doh-nah noh-bees pah-chem*\\
(Latin) "Give us peace." There is a popular hymn by this name that is often sung in the round.

(la) donna è mobile *la doh-nah ee moh-bee-ley*\\
(Italian) It is hard to see this line without singing the aria from Verdi's *Rigoletto*. It means "women are fickle."

doppelgänger *do-pel-gang-er*\\
(German) A double or look-alike.

double entendre *doo-ble en-tahn-dru*\\
(French) "Double" is pronounced *doo-ble*\\, but English speakers tend to use their normal pronunciation in the first word of this expression, which refers to a word or phrase that has two different interpretations, one *risqué*.

dramatis personae *dra-ma-tis per-soh-ney*\\
(Latin) The list of characters at the beginning of a theatrical script.

dreidel *drey-del*\\
(Yiddish) A top used in a game played on Hanukkah.

D

dressage \dre-sahzh\
(French) Horse training.

duende \doo-end-ey\
(Spanish) A dark, overwhelming source of creative inspiration.
This sense of the word, which also refers to a ghost or goblin,
was popularized by the Spanish poet Federico García Lorca.

du jour \doo zhoor\
(French) "Of the day." It is used on menus to indicate a daily
special, as in "soup *du jour*"; also for anything ephemeral,
such as "the pop star *du jour*."

dummkopf \doom-kof\
(German) An idiot, a dummy. The amusing literal translation is
"dumb head."

dum spiro spero \dum spee-roh spe-roh\
(Latin) A motto of South Carolina, which translates to "While I
breathe, I hope."

dura mater \doo-rah mah-ter\
(Latin) "Strong mother." The tough outer membrane that
encases the brain and spinal cord.

duvet \doo-vey\
(French) A down comforter.

eau de cologne \\oh de koh-lohn\\
(French) "Water from Cologne," Germany. A fragrance that is cheaper than perfume but still makes you smell nice.

eau de toilette \\oh de twah-let\\
(French) It means "toilet water" but it is not the stuff in the bowl. Rather, it is diluted perfume.

éclat \\ey-klah\\
(French) A word that means both brilliant success and the acclaim that comes with it.

écru \\ey-kroo\\
(French) Usually spelled without the accent mark. This is a beige-y sort of color. Its name refers to unbleached linen.

edelweiss \\ey-del-veyes\\
(German) In German, the name of this alpine flower is properly spelled *Edelweiß*. The component parts of the word are "noble" and "white." Thanks to the popularity of *The Sound of Music*, many people believe the song "Edelweiss" is an old Austrian folk song. It is not; it was written in 1959.

effleurage \e-floor-ahzh\
(French) A gentle rubbing technique used in massage.

ego \ee-goh\
(Latin) *Ego* is "I" in Latin. After a couple thousand years of me, me, me, the word began to take on a sense of self-focus and conceit in the 1890s.

ego te absolvo \ee-goh tey ahb-zol-voh\
(Latin) "I absolve you." From the Sacrament of Penance in the Roman Catholic Church.

ei incumbit probatio qui dicit, non qui negat
   \ey in-kum-bit pro-bah-tee-yoh kwee dee-kit\
   nahn kwee neh-got
(Latin) This is a long-winded Latin way of saying "the burden of proof lies on he who affirms, not he who denies," or "innocent until proven guilty."

einfühlung \ayn-foo-lung\
(German) "One feeling"; that is to say, "empathy."

élan vital \ey-lahn vee-tahl\
(French) Essential energy. (See page 174.)

GREEK VS. FRENCH
EXCLAMATIONS!

EUREKA!

The Greek *eureka*, meaning "I have found it," was supposedly shouted by Archimedes after he stepped into his bath and noticed that the water level rose. He was so excited by his discovery about fluid dynamics that he went running through the streets naked to tell everyone about it.

VOILÀ!

Voilà, meaning "see there," is less scientific but a tad more sunny and optimistic. It refers to something pleasant that has happened as if by magic.

THE WINNER?

The Greek word has the benefit of a built-in scientific anecdote, but the French can be applied in almost any situation. One point to the French.

El Niño \el neen-yoh\

(Spanish) A warm ocean current that causes extreme weather. Supposedly named by Peruvian fishermen who noticed that conditions were bad every few years around Christmas. *Niño* means "boy" but *El Niño* refers to the Christ child.

embouchure \ahn-boo-shur\

(French) The mouthpiece of a woodwind or brass instrument (except those with double reeds); also the position in which a musician holds the lips to play the instrument.

embonpoint /ahn-bawn-pwan/

(French) Plumpness, but literally "in good health." (See page 230.)

embusqué \ahn-boos-key\

(French) A person who takes a government job or academic position in order to avoid military service.

éminence grise \ey-mee-nons greez\

(French) An agent who wields influence behind the scenes.

emoji \ee-moh-jee\

(Japanese) Cartoon icons representing emotions used in texting.

enceinte \on-sent\

(French) An ultra-polite way to refer to pregnancy. It was

famously the term approved by the television network censors to refer to Lucille Ball's pregnancy on *I Love Lucy*. *Enceinte* literally means "without a girdle."

enchanté \on-shon-tey\
(French) A pretentious way to say "Pleased to meet you."

enfant gâté \on-fahn gah-tey\
(French) A spoiled child, or someone who behaves like one.

enfant terrible \on-fahn te-ree-ble\
(French) Someone who behaves like a terrible child, for example someone whose behavior is a public embarrassment. Often applied to celebrities who try to draw attention by being shocking.

enfilade \ahn-fi-luhd\
(French) Things positioned in a straight line. Once used to describe lines of trees or rows of apartments, eventually, it became primarily a military term referring to firing on the length of an enemy position.

en garde \on gahrd\
(French) Just like it sounds, this phrase means "on guard." It is called out at the beginning of a round of fencing and is the most civilized way to say "Get ready, I'm going to attack you."

E

en masse \on mahs\
(French) As a group.

ennui \on-wee\
(French) A feeling of melancholy, listlessness. Mild depression with a *soupçon* of world-weariness. (See page 78.)

ennuyé \on-wee-ey\
(French) A person who embodies the type of designer boredom often associated with teenagers. Someone who is totes not impressed.

en prise \on preez\
(French) In chess terminology, a piece is *en prise* when it is unguarded and can be taken by an opponent.

entrepreneur \on-tre-pre-nur\
(French) Originally as used in English, an entrepreneur was a theatrical manager. That sense has vanished. Now it means a person who takes the risk of starting a small business.

épater les bourgeois \ey-pah-tey ley boor-zhwah\
(French) To shock and amaze complacent, polite society.

épée \ey-pey\
(French) A fencing term for a light dueling sword without sharp edges.

e pluribus unum \ee *plur-i-bus oo-num*\
(Latin) "Out of the many, one." You will find this on the Great
Seal of the United States.

ergo \er-goh\
(Latin) Therefore.

Erin go bragh! \e-rin goh brah\
(Irish Gaelic) Ireland forever!

errata \e-rah-tah\
(Latin) Mistakes. Used in publishing for a list of corrections
inserted into a published text

ersatz \er-sahts\
(German) An imitation, an inferior copy.

espionage \es-pee-oh-nahzh\
(French) Spying.

esprit de corps \e-spree de cor\
(French) Teamwork. The spirit of working together as
one body.

esprit de l'escalier \e-spree de les-kahl-ee-ey\
(French) A clever rejoinder that comes after the conversation
is finished. (See page 205.)

FRENCH VS. GERMAN
DEPRESSION

ENNUI

This French word literally means "boredom" and it describes a state of existential disappointment with the world, especially as experienced by filmmakers and poets.

WELTSCHMERZ

Germans are not immune to melancholy. *Weltschmerz* means "world-weariness." It describes the kind of alienation and heaviness caused by the gap between how the world is and how it ought to be. The Germans have such high hopes for the world, and yet it keeps letting them down.

THE WINNER?

The French are not amused by life. The Germans are actively disappointed in it. There is a bit more idealism underlying the German *weltanschauung*, but sometimes you're in the mood to watch a poet stare straight into the camera while a single tear escapes down his cheek. This one goes to the French.

esse quam videri \es-se *kwahm vi-de-ree*\
(Latin) "To be, rather than to seem." The state motto of North Carolina.

estro poetico \es-*troh poh-e-tee-koh*\
(Italian) The poetic imagination.

et alia \et *al-ee-ah*\
(Latin) "And others." Abbreviated *et al.* You will often find it in footnotes when authors or editors are listed, in which context it often means "The scholar who got all the credit and a bunch of other people who did all the grunt work."

et cetera \et *set-er-ah*\
(Latin) And so on, and so on, and so forth.

l'étoile du Nord \ley-*twahl doo nor*\
(French) "The star of the North." The state motto of Minnesota.

eureka \you-*reek-ah*\
(Greek) An interjection meaning "I have found it!" (See page 73.)

excelsior \ek-*sel-see-or*\
(Latin) "Higher." This is a popular name for hotels and also the state motto of New York.

exegesis \ek-sah-jee-sis\
(Greek) An examination of a text.

exempli gratia \eg-zem-plee grah-tee-ah\
(Latin) For example. It's what the abbreviation *e.g.* stands for.

exeunt \ek-sey-ent\
(Latin) The third-person plural present indicative form of *exire* "to exit" is used these days almost entirely as a theatrical stage direction meaning "the whole group leaves the stage."

ex libris \eks *lee-bris*\
(Latin) Written on a bookplate to indicate whose library the book was stolen from.

ex parte \eks *pahr-tey*\
(Latin) A legal decision that is made with only one of the parties to the dispute present.

ex post facto \eks *post fak-to*\
(Latin) "From after the fact." A legal decision that affects issues that existed before the enactment of the law.

façade \fah-sahd\

(French) The exterior, public-facing, and therefore the most decorated, part of a building. By extension, a false persona that conceals inner emotion or motives.

fahrvergnügen \fahr-fer-noo-gen\

(German) Driving pleasure. The word was popularized by a Volkswagen commercial. (*Volkswagen*, incidentally, means "people's car.")

fait accompli \feyt a-kom-plee\

(French) A done deal.

falsetto \fahl-set-oh\

(Italian) Singing in a range above the natural register.

fandango \fan-dang-goh\

(Spanish) A South American dance performed to guitar accompaniment by a pair of dancers. Also, a necessary word for singing the first line of Procol Harum's "A Whiter Shade of Pale." (*Procol Harum*, incidentally, is the Latin for "beyond these things" as written by someone who didn't pay much attention in Latin class: the cases of the two words do not match.)

TAINTED GERMAN

One unfortunate way that cultures come into contact is through war, and a number of German words and phrases became familiar, and infamous, from their use by the Nazi regime in World War II. Before Adolf Hitler, the word *Führer* was mostly used to refer to a guide (such as a tour guide) or in combination with a political party as in "the leader of the Socialist party." Hitler referred to himself simply as "the leader" in order to build a cult of personality around himself. The word is now associated almost entirely with Hitler, and modern Germans use the words *Anführer* or *Leiter* instead. The words that accompanied the straight-armed salute of the *Führer*, "*Sieg Heil*!" translate to "hail victory." The phrase and salute are now considered illegal propaganda in Germany, and some terms that seem entirely innocuous out of context have been banned as hate speech in Germany, including *die Fahne hoch*, "the flag on high," part of the opening line of the Nazi anthem, and *Mit deutschem Gruß*, "with German greetings," which was how high-ranking Nazi officers signed their correspondence.

fartlek *fart-lek*\
(Swedish) A method of training for runners involving periods of intense physical activity interspersed with periods of lower effort.

fatwa *fah-twah*\
(Arabic) Although it is sometimes assumed to mean harsh condemnation or a death sentence, a *fatwa* is simply a ruling by a recognized authority on a point of Islamic law.

faux *foh*\
(French) Fake. Imitation. Artificial.

faux pas *foh pah*\
(French) A false step, a mistake.

femme *fem*\
(French) Woman.

femme fatale *fem fey-tahl*\
(French) A dangerous but seductive woman.

feng shui *feng shwey*\
(Chinese) The art of arranging furniture and structural objects in a home or office to maximize the flow of *chi* (see entry for *qi*).

F

fermata \fer-mah-tah\
(Italian) In musical notation, a symbol above a note indicating that it is to be held longer than usual.

ferula \fer-oo-lah\
(Latin) The word means "rod" and refers to the staff used by the Pope on ceremonial occasions.

fez \fez\
(Turkish) A flat-topped, round, brimless hat worn by men in the eastern Mediterranean and by Shriners.

fiasco \fee-as-koh\
(Italian) A stunning failure, a complete disaster. The word derives from the Italian for "flask" and alludes to a glassblower trying to perform the delicate task of creating such an object. If the craftsman made a mistake, it would smash in spectacular fashion.

fin de siècle \fen de see-e-kle\
(French) The end of the century, usually the nineteenth.

fjord \fee-ord\
(Norwegian) A long, narrow inlet between steep cliffs.

flambé \flahm-bey\
(French) A dish covered in liquor and set on fire.

flatus *flah-tus*\
(Latin) "Blowing." Expelled intestinal gas.

flense *flens*\
(Danish) To strip the blubber from an animal's skin (usually a whale's.) Though literal usage is uncommon, corporate types have found metaphorical use for it during layoffs.

fleur-de-lis *flur de lee*\
(French) The rather redundantly named "flower of the lily" is a stylized image of such a three-petaled plant used in art or heraldry.

flügelhorn *floo-gel-horn*\
(German) A musical instrument similar to a trumpet.

folie à deux *foh-lee ah du*\
(French) A delusional belief system shared simultaneously by two closely associated people.

folie de doute *foh-lee de doot*\
(French) Used in psychology, an obsessive-compulsive disorder in which a person suffers from excessive doubt.

force majeure *fors mah-jur*\
(French) In law, unforeseen circumstances that prevent a party from being able to complete a contractual obligation.

F

forme fruste *form froost*\
(French) A medical term for an incomplete or atypical
expression of a disease or illness.

fortissimo *for-tee-see-moh*\
(Italian) A musical passage played with force, loudly.

frappé *fra-pey*\
(French) To whip or strike. This is used to describe drinks
made with crushed ice. It is also ballet terminology for a
quick motion with the foot.

fräulein *frow-layn*\
(German) A young, unmarried German woman.

frou-frou *froo froo*\
(French) From the word for the rustling sound of silk fabric
comes a term for anything fancy, frilly, and affected.

fruits de mer *free de mer*\
(French) "Fruit of the sea." Seafood.

frum *frum*\
(Yiddish) An adjective describing a religiously observant Jew.

CUT ME SOME FLAK

Why do we use the word "flak" for an anti-aircraft gun (and metaphorically for being shot down with criticism)? Because the German *Fliegerabwehrkanone* is just too much word. It's one of those wonderful German compound nouns that literally means "pilot-warding-off cannon."

führer \fyoor-er\
(German) This now-tainted word translates literally to "leader." (See page 82.)

fusillade \fyoo-sil-ahd\
(French) Simultaneous discharge of multiple rifles. It is sometimes used metaphorically for a bombardment of criticism.

futon \foo-tahn\
(Japanese) A padded mattress without springs that can be folded into a seat.

gaffe \gaf\
(French) A blunder or mistake, particularly one with embarrassing social repercussions.

galactico \ga-lak-tik-oh\
(Spanish) "A person from another galaxy." A soccer (football) superstar who draws a huge salary. The term is closely associated with the team Real Madrid.

gan bei \gahn bey\
(Chinese) A common Chinese toast that literally means "dry the cup." English-speaking ex-pats in China use *gan bei* as a synonym for getting drunk. For example, "He was a little bit worse for wear after a long night of *gan bei*–ing."

ganja \gahn-jah\
(Hindi) Marijuana.

garçon \gahr-sohn\
(French) In English, it would be rude to summon a waiter by calling out "boy" but this is, indeed, what you do in France and in snooty French restaurants.

gauche \gohsh\

(French) *Gauche* is the French word for "left." In English it came to mean something clumsy, as when a right-handed person tries to write with the left. Eventually, it took on a sense of being not only clumsy but tacky and ill-mannered. (See also *louche*.)

gaucho \gow-choh\

(Spanish) A South American cowboy.

(les) Gaulois \gahl-wah\

(French) During the Roman Empire, Gaul was the name of a geographical region that now largely consists of France. The people of the region were *Gaulois*, and so it is sometimes used as a synonym for the French. *Gauloise* (with an *e* because cigarettes are feminine in French) is also a famous brand of cigarette popular with countercultural types.

geisha \gey-shah\

(Japanese) A woman trained in music, dance, and conversation, who serves as a professional hostess and companion.

gemeinschaft \ge-mayn-shahft\

(German) Social relations based on close family ties. (As contrasted with *gesellschaft*; see entry.)

gemütlichkeit \ge-moot-lik-kayt\
(German) A cozy and comfortable place. A warm sense of belonging.

gendarme \zhahn-dahrm\
(French) A French paramilitary police officer.

genius loci \jee-nee-us loh-kee\
(Latin) The atmosphere or feeling of a place. It was originally a reference to the gods who protected a location.

gentilhomme \zhen-tee-ohm\
(French) A gentleman.

gesellschaft \ge-zel-shaft\
(German) A society in which people pursue their own interests without focusing on the good of the community as a whole.

gestalt \ge-stahlt\
(German) The notion that the whole has an independent existence beyond its individual parts.

gestapo \ges-tah-poh\
(German) German secret police during the Nazi era, used more broadly for a police force or authority figure that uses strong-arm tactics.

gesundheit \ge-zund-hayt\
(German) In German, it means "health," and in many parts of the English-speaking world, it means someone just sneezed.

ghetto \ge-toh\
(Italian) Originally, it referred to a restricted area where Jews were required to live. Now expanded to refer to any area where marginalized people are concentrated.

gigolo \jee-goh-loh\
(French) A professional male escort.

glasnost \glaz-nost\
(Russian) An official policy of greater openness and freedom of information, refers specifically to the last years of the Soviet Union.

glaube dem leben \glow-be dem lee ben\
(German) Have faith in life.

glockenspiel \glok-en-shpeel\
(German) A musical instrument consisting of metal bars.

gondola \gon-doh-lah\
(Italian) A flat-bottom boat used on the canals of Venice. The person who steers such a craft is a *gondolier*.

FRENCH VS. SPANISH

THE MACABRE

FRENCH

Before there were horror films, France had the *Grand Guignol*. It was sensational, gory, and over-the-top, and audiences loved to be horrified by it. *Grand Guignol* is a term that you could use, were you so inclined, to describe *Nightmare on Elm Street*.

SPANISH

The Spanish *duende* is more Edgar Allan Poe than *I Know What You Did Last Summer*. *Duende* is a deep spiritual appreciation of the dark, earthy side of artistic expression. As described by the poet Federico García Lorca, it is an irrational demon that is linked to passion and the awareness of death.

THE WINNER?

Chacun à son goût. For the dark, guilty pleasure of being scared out of your pants with some low-brow entertainment, you have to go with les *Français*. If you have a touch of poetry in your soul, it's a point for Spain.

gonif *gon-if*\
(Yiddish) A swindler, someone you can't trust.

götterdämmerung *got-er-de-me-rung*\
(German) The downfall of the gods, meaning the collapse of a powerful political regime. Also the name of a famous Wagner opera.

Gott sei dank! *got zay dahnk*\
(German) Thank god!

gourmand *goor-mahnd*\
(French) A person who enjoys food and a lot of it.

gourmet *goor-mey*\
(French) A person who has highly elevated taste in *cuisine*.

graffiti *grah-fee-tee*\
(Italian) Writing on public walls done without permission. *Graffiti* is the plural of *graffito*, although it is hard to envision what a single unit of wall writing is.

grammatici certant *gra-ma-tee-chee ser-tent*\
(Latin) A dispute between grammarians. More broadly, it means a problem that experts continue to debate and have not resolved.

Grand Guignol *grahn gee-nyol*\

(French) "Big puppet." It is an allusion to a Parisian puppet theater of that name, which specialized in the gruesome and macabre. By extension, any dark and disturbing entertainment.

grand mal *grahn mahl*\

(French) "Large sickness." A *grand mal* seizure is also known as a generalized tonic-clonic seizure. It involves a loss of consciousness and violent muscle contractions. (See also *petit mal*.)

grand prix *grahn pree*\

(French) "The great prize." The first contest referred to as a *grand prix* in English was a horse race. Now it usually refers to auto racing.

grande dame *grahn dahm*\

(French) A great lady. Usually a highly respected woman of high society.

graviora manent *grah-vor-ah ma-nent*\

(Latin) A cheery little phrase meaning "the worst is yet to come."

gravitas *grah-vee-tahs*\

(Latin) Seriousness, dignity.

GURU OF THE BEATLES
JAI GURU DEVA OM
\\jeye goo-roo day-vuh ohm\\

This line from the Beatles song "Across the Universe" is a *mantra* that means roughly, "Hail wise teacher Dev." The literal translation of *jai* is "victory" and was a word used to salute heroes returning from battle. Guru Dev was a real person. He was a wandering mystic and the teacher of Maharishi Mahesh Yogi, with whom the Beatles were studying when John Lennon wrote this song. (See also *om*.)

gringo \\gring-goh\\
(Spanish) A mildly offensive term for a non-Hispanic person.

(la) grippe \\grip\\
(French) The French word for the flu, it is what the upper classes used to call it when they got stuffy noses. Sometimes anglicized to "the grip."

G

guano *gwah-noh*\
(Mexican Spanish) Bird or bat dung.

gulag *goo-log*\
(Russian) A Soviet prison camp, sometimes used as a general synonym for "jail."

gung ho *gung hoh*\
(Chinese) "Work together." It was adopted as a slogan by a division of World War II marines stationed in China, and the expression became associated with the young soldiers' bravery and enthusiasm.

guru *goo-roo*\
(Sanskrit) In Indian religions, a wise teacher or master. Applied conversationally to anyone who is an expert, for example a "financial guru." (See page 95.)

gutta-percha *gut-ah per-chah*\
(Malaysian) Latex derived from certain Malaysian trees. Mostly used as a dental splint.

habeas corpus \hey-bee-us kor-pus\
(Latin) "You shall have the body." A writ requiring that a prisoner appear in court to determine if detention is legal.

habitué \ha-bit-choo-ey\
(French) A person who is a regular at a particular place. "Norm is a *habitué* of Cheers."

haboob \ha-boob\
(Arabic) A dust storm. These occur in desert regions when the downdrafts from nearby thunderstorms pick up and scatter sand, reducing visibility to near zero. (See page 104.)

hacienda \hah-see-en-dah\
(Spanish) A large, Spanish-style estate house.

haiku \hay-koo\
(Japanese) A form of verse written in lines of five, seven, and five syllables, usually with nature and seasons as its subject.

hajj \haj\
(Arabic) The Muslim pilgrimage to the Sacred Mosque at Mecca. A *hajji* is a Muslim who has performed the hajj.

Hoi Polloi

THE UNWASHED MASSES OR THE SNOOTY SNOBS?

The original meaning of *hoi polloi* is "the many," the bulk of people in contrast to the elites.

It was used by those who liked to look down their noses at commoners while describing them using the ancient languages they gleaned from their classical educations.

But "*hoi polloi*" sounds like it ought to describe the hoity-toity, and over time, this misusage has become common enough to be acknowledged by some dictionaries. The *New Fowler's Modern English Usage* reports on the secondary sense, and gives some examples of its appearance in print, but calls it an "unwelcome use."

hakuna matata *hah-koo-nah mah-tah-tah*\
(Swahili) A phrase meaning "there are no worries." Used primarily to sing a song from Disney's *The Lion King*.

halal *halal*\
(Arabic) Prepared according to Muslim dietary laws.

hallelujah *hah-ley-loo-yah*\
(Latin) "Hail god." The last part of the word, the "yah," is a shortened form of *Yahweh*.

hara-kiri *hah-rah kee-ree*\
(Japanese) Ritual suicide by self-disemboweling with a ceremonial knife. English speakers often mispronounce this as *har-ee kar-ee*\.

hare *hah-rey*\
(Sanskrit) "Hail!" *Hare Krishna* means "hail to (the Hindu god) Krishna."

hashish *hah-sheesh*\
(Arabic) A drug made from Indian hemp.

hasta la muerte todo es vida
   ahs-tah luh mwer-tey toh-doh es vee-dah\
(Spanish) "Until death, all is life." The equivalent of "Where there's life, there's hope."

hasta la vista \ahs-tah lah vee-stah\
(Spanish) Until we meet again. The Spanish equivalent of the French *au revoir*, baby.

hausfrau \hows-frow\
(German) A housewife.

haute couture \oht koo-toor\
(French) High fashion.

hentai \hen-tay\
(Japanese) A Japanese word for sexual perversion that is used internationally to describe sexually explicit *anime* and *manga*.

heresiarch \he-res-ee-ark\
(Latin) A leader of a heretical sect. One who promotes heresies.

hijab \hi-jahb\
(Arabic) *Hijab* means "to cover," but it is also used to describe a veil or headscarf worn by Muslim women in public.

himmel \hi-mel\
(German) "Heaven." Often uttered as an exclamation.

hinterland \hin-ter-land\
(German) An inland area behind a coastline. Used colloquially to describe a rural place far from everything.

COWBOY SPANGLISH

HOOSEGOW

"Hoosegow" is a quaint old Western word for "jail." It comes from the mangled spelling of the Spanish *juzgao* ("jail") which ultimately came from *juzgado*, meaning "a courtroom." In those days, the courtroom and the jail were often in the same building. In the old days, before spelling was as standardized as it is today, you could find all manner of spellings of this word.

Other words borrowed from Spanish by cowboys who didn't know how to spell the language include "huckaroo" (*vaquero*), "lasso" (*lazo*), "lariat" (*la reata*), and "chaps" (*chapparreras*).

hoi polloi *hoi poh-loi*\\
(Greek) "The many." A mildly derogatory term for the masses. In speech, it can sometimes mean the exact opposite. *Hoi* is Greek for "the." Therefore "the *hoi polloi*," as it is often used, means "the the many." (See page 98.)

honcho *hahn-choh*\

(Japanese) The top dog. The boss. Usually paired with the word "head."

honoris causa *oh-nor-is kow-zah*\

(Latin) "For the sake of honor."

hookah *hoo-kah*\

(Arabic) A water pipe with a long, flexible tube through which tobacco smoke is drawn.

hoopla *hoop-lah*\

(French) The French use this as an exclamation when someone does an impressive trick. For example, a circus ring master might shout "*Hoop-la!*" after an acrobat does a flip. Because of the association with flashy tricks, *hoopla* has come to mean any overblown excitement.

hors de combat *or de kom-ba*\

(French) "Out of combat." Refers to an injured soldier who is taken out of action.

hubris *hyoo-bris*\

(Greek) Excessive pride and overconfidence. Usually used to describe the kind of pride that goeth before destruction.

HUNGARIAN VS. JAPANESE
WARRIORS

HUSSAR

The *hussars* were cavalry men, and they were nothing if not sharp dressers. They wore those gold-braided, waist-length jackets that in a later age, rock stars would adopt. (Think Michael Jackson in the 1980s.) Speeding on horseback with bayonets outstretched, they led Napoleon's troops into battle and conquered much of Europe.

NINJA

Ninjas were no slouches either. They were secret agents, spies, and mercenaries trained in the art of stealth. Dressed all in black and sporting shortened samurai swords, they were rumored to have a secret walk that allowed them to move faster than anyone else.

THE WINNER?

Give this round to the Hungarians. A crafty *ninja* hiding in the woods would be a formidable foe, but the *hussars* had the advantage of horses and a whole army behind them.

XENOPHOBIA AND LINGUISTIC BORROWING

The word *haboob* describes a dust storm in a desert region. They are common features of certain parts of Africa and the Middle East. When a dramatic mile-high wall of dust darkened the skies of Phoenix, some residents objected to the use of an Arabic name for a made-in-America storm. "I am insulted that local TV news crews are now calling this kind of storm a *haboob*," one resident wrote to the *Arizona Republic*. "How do they think our soldiers feel coming back to Arizona and hearing some Middle Eastern term?"

huevos \hwey-vohs\
(Spanish) Literally, "eggs." Figuratively, *cojones*.

hussar \hoo-zahr\
(Hungarian) A member of the Hungarian light cavalry or a similar unit of well-dressed European horsemen. (In Hungarian, it is spelled *huszár*. See page 103.)

ibidem \i-bi-dem\

(Latin) You will find this word or its abbreviation *ibid.* in the footnotes of books. It means "in the same place" and refers to a work by an author cited in the previous note.

ichiban \i-chee-bahn\

(Japanese) Number one. The best. A common name for Japanese restaurants.

id \id\

(Latin) *Id* is "it" in Latin. In 1924, Joan Riviere's translated Sigmund Freud's *Das Ich und das Es* ("The I and the It") using the Latin words *ego* and *id*. The *id* is the unconscious driving force behind the *ego*. (See page 111.)

idée fixe \ee-dey feeks\

(French) A "fixed idea," an obsession.

id est \id est\

(Latin) Because scholars need a fancy term for "that is." Most often, you'll see this abbreviated to *i.e.*

ignoratio elenchi *ig-nor-ah-tee-oh e-len-kee*\\
(Latin) This is a term that should be more often used by media figures when interviewing politicians. It is an argument that might be true, but has nothing to do with the subject being discussed.

ignotum per ignotius *ig-noh-tum per ig-noh-tee-us*\\
(Latin) "The unknown by the more unknown," an explanation which is even more obscure than that which it is supposed to explain.

imam *ee-mahm*\\
(Arabic) Shiite Muslim religious leader who claims direct descent from Mohammed.

imbroglio *im-brohl-yoh*\\
(Italian) A bitter and complex misunderstanding or difficult situation; a real mess.

impresario *im-pres-ahr-ee-oh*\\
(Italian) A theatrical manager or organizer.

imprimatur *im-pree-mah-ter*\\
(Latin) From the term for a license given by the Roman Catholic Church to print a religious work comes a word that now means any expression of official approval.

impromptu \im-promp-too\

(French) An event put together on the spur of the moment without advance planning. A theatrical or musical performance.

in absentia \in ab-sen-chah\

(Latin) Not there.

inamorata \in-a-mor-ah-tah\

(Italian) If you're looking for a more artful word for your significant other, girlfriend, partner, lover, you might use this. The masculine version is *inamorato*.

in articulo mortis \in ahr-tik-yoo-loh mor-tis\

(Latin) A legal term that means "in the grasp of death." It refers to a statement made by someone who had nothing to gain or lose anymore because he or she was about to kick the bucket.

in bocca al lupo \in boh-kah al loop-oh\

(Italian) It means "into the jaws of the wolf" and is an expression sometimes used by superstitious thespians in place of "good luck" in the same way they use "break a leg!"

in camera \in kam-e-rah\

(Latin) A legal proceeding conducted in the judge's chambers rather than in open court.

incommunicado \in ko-myoo-ni-kah-doh\
(Spanish) Out of communication.

inconnu \in-ko-noo\
(French) "Unknown." Often a person whom is uknown; a
stranger.

index librorum prohibitorum
   \in-deks lib-ror-um proh-hi-bi-tor-um\
(Latin) The Roman Catholic Church's official list of prohibited
books. The list was abandoned in 1966. By then, it had
become more of a recommended reading list.

in excelsis \in ek-sel-sees\
(Latin) "In the highest." *Gloria in excelsis Deo* is "glory to God
in the highest."

in extremis \in eks-trem-is\
(Latin) In an extremely dire situation.

inflagrante delicto \in-flah-grahn-tey de-lik-toh\
(Latin) "In blazing offense." Caught in the act.

infundibulum \in-fun-dib-yoo-lum\
(Latin) The Latin word for "funnel" is used in English for
funnel-shaped anatomical structures, including the outermost

section of the fallopian tubes, a formation in the brain, and a structure in the cochlea of the ear. (See sidebar.)

ingénue \on-zhey-noo\
(French) A young woman who is sweet, innocent, and a bit naïve. In English, it is usually spelled without the accent mark.

in loco parentis \in loh-koh pahr-en-tis\
(Latin) "In the place of parents." A stand-in for a parent.

in medias res \in may-dee-ahs reyz\
(Latin) A literary term term for a scene that opens mid-action.

in memoriam \in me-mor-ee-ahm\
(Latin) "In memory."

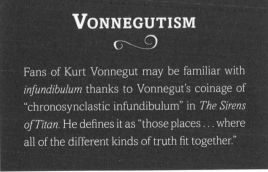

VONNEGUTISM

Fans of Kurt Vonnegut may be familiar with *infundibulum* thanks to Vonnegut's coinage of "chronosynclastic infundibulum" in *The Sirens of Titan*. He defines it as "those places . . . where all of the different kinds of truth fit together."

innuendo \in-yoo-en-doh\

(Latin) *Innuendo* entered our language as a strictly legal term. It translates as "giving a nod to" and means a thinly veiled suggestion of impropriety.

insha' Allah \in-shah ah-lah\

(Arabic) "God willing."

in situ \in si-too\

(Latin) In its natural environment. Used by scholars when they go out in the field to study animals, archaeological objects, *et cetera*.

in toto \in toh-toh\

(Latin) Totally.

in utero \in yoo-ter-oh\

(Latin) "In the uterus." A baby that has not yet been born.

invictus \in-vik-tus\

(Latin) "Unconquered." It is the title of a famous poem by the poet William Ernest Henley. You may know its last lines: "I am the master of my fate: / I am the captain of my soul."

in vino veritas \in vee-noh ver-ee-tahs\

(Latin) "In wine there is truth." Refers to the things you're too restrained to say without a bit of the grape.

Latin vs. Latin
UNCONSCIOUS TEMPTATIONS

SUCCUBUS

We can assume that it was quite early in human history when people first observed a particular phenomenon of the psyche: People sometimes have vivid erotic dreams. In medieval times, these uncontrollable phenomena were explained by demons. The *succubus* was a demonic temptress who had her way with men in their sleep. Female visitors were visited by the *incubus*.

ID

In the early twentieth century Sigmund Freud turned his attention to erotic night visions. Freud did not attribute them to anything supernatural. Instead, he posited that there was an unconscious force which was responsible for instinctual drives. This concept was translated into English with the Latin word for "it," *id*.

THE WINNER?

Personally, I find the idea of a wandering erotic spirit doing mischief in the night to be much more poetic than Freud's theory. I am going to give this one to the *succubus*.

ipecac *i-pi-kak*\\
(indigenous Brazilian) A shortened form of *ipecacuanha*, a medicine used to induce vomiting.

ipso facto *ip-soh fak-toh*\\
(Latin) In and of itself, therefore. According to Law.com, it is a phrase more popular with comedians imitating lawyers than by lawyers themselves.

LATIN SPELLED BADLY
JINX

The ancient Romans used to warn people to beware of the *iynx*, a bird that was believed to be used by witches to cast magic spells. That was a long time ago, and over the years, people forgot all about the bird. They did remember the sound of *iynx*, although they had started to spell it *jinx*. They also knew that it was something that caused bad luck. The word didn't make its way into English, however, until 1911.

j'accuse \zha-kooz\
(French) "I accuse!"

j'adoube \zhah-doob\
(French) "I adjust." A bit of chess terminology. It is when a player touches a piece with no intention of moving it.

jai alai \heye ah-leye\
(Spanish) A game played with a ball and large, curved wicker baskets.

jalousie \zhan-loo-see\
(French) A poetic French way of saying "jealousy."

jamais de ma vie \zhah-mey de mah vee\
(French) "Never in my life."

jawohl \yah-vol\
(German) Yes, of course.

jejune \je-joon\
(Latin) Childish and uninformed.

je me souviens *zheh meh soo-vee-en*\

(French) "I remember." The motto of Quebec. (See also *souvenir.*)

je ne sais quoi *zhe ne sey kwah*\

(French) Someone that has a certain "I don't know what." A captivating quality that's hard to pin down but you know it when you see it.

jeunesse dorée *zhe-nes dor-ey*\

(French) "Golden youth." Refers to rich and fashionable young people.

jihad *jee-hahd*\

(Arabic) A spiritual struggle. The word, in itself, does not connote violence or military action, nor is it a declaration of war against other religions.

jodhpurs *jod-purz*\

(Hindi) Riding trousers cut wide at the hip.

jojoba *hoh-hoh-bah*\

(Spanish) A green shrub found in the southwestern United States that produces an oil used widely in cosmetics.

jonquil *zhon-kwil*\\

(French) The jonquil is a species of narcissus. Its name comes to English with a slight change in spelling from the French *jonquille*. The French got the word from the Latin *juncus*, and it was originally pronounced *junk wil*\\. Thinking this was a bit of an ugly name for a pretty flower, the pronunciation shifted to the more euphonious *zhon kwil*\\.

judo *joo-doh*\\

(Japanese) A Japanese martial art that is a modern variant of *jujitsu*. *Judo* means "the gentle way."

jujitsu *joo-jit-soo*\\

(Japanese) A Japanese martial art without weapons.

julienne *zhoo-lee-en*\\

(French) To cut vegetables into thin strips.

junta *hoon-tah*\\

(Spanish) A political group seeking power.

justia omnibus *yoost-ee-ah om-ni-bus*\\

(Latin) "Justice for all."

When Two Cultures Meet
THAT JOLLY JUMBUCK

The "jumbuck" that the "swagman" put in his "tucker bag" in the song "Waltzing Matilda" was a sheep. The swagman is an itinerant worker. Tucker is food, thus a tucker bag is a food sack. The word "jumbuck" appears to come neither from an aboriginal language nor English. Instead it was coined out of both as the two groups tried to communicate with each other about the imported animal.

These kinds of simplified mutual languages are called "pidgin." Some etymologists suggest "jumbuck" might be an aboriginal version of an English phrase like "jump up." (Although why you'd call a sheep a "jump up" when you are surrounded by kangaroos is something of a mystery to this author.)

The kangaroo, an animal previously unknown to Europeans, supposedly got its name when Captain James Cook asked a native what the animal's name was. The native supposedly responded "*Kangaroo*," meaning "I don't know," and Cook thought that's what the animal was called. Most etymologists think that anecdote, although popular and fun, has no basis in fact.

The name for a small kangaroo is a "wallaby," and that does derive from a native language. The locals called it a *wolaba*. The koala was also named by the locals, but they called it a *kulla* or *koola*.

When two linguistic traditions live side by side for an extended period, a pidgin language can evolve into a full-fledged common tongue. Such languages are called "creoles." Gullah is a creole of several West African languages brought by slaves to the Sea Islands off of the Carolina coast. In Gullah, *jook* or *joog* means "wicked." The term ultimately traces its origin (in a changed form) to either Bambara, a language of Gambia, or Wolof, the national language of Senegal.

The Gullah term *jook house* was used to describe places where people behaved in wild, wicked ways—gaming parlors, brothels, and dance halls. Many of these places were equipped with new devices that were once described with cumbersome names such as "nickel-in-the-slot phonographs." By the late 1930s, everyone was calling them "jukeboxes."

kabuki \kah-boo-kee\
(Japanese) A Japanese form of highly stylized theater.

kaddish \kah-dish\
(Aramaic) A Jewish prayer used in the synagogue and in mourning rituals.

kaffeeklatsch \kah-fey-klach\
(German) A gossipy get-together over coffee.

kaftan \kaf-tan\
(Turkish) A long, belted tunic worn by men in the Near East.

kahuna \kah-hoo-nah\
(Indigenous Hawaiian) The top person, the one in charge. The head *honcho*. Originally a *kahuna* was an expert in folk medicine.

kaiser \kay-zer\
(German) *Kaiser* is, like the Russian *czar*, another word for "Caesar."

kaizen *kay-zen*\\

(Japanese) A Japanese management concept based on continuous, incremental improvement.

kanban *kahn-bahn*\\

(Japanese) A just-in-time inventory management process. It comes from a word meaning "billboard" or card used to tell a producer what parts are needed.

karaoke *ka-ree-oh-kee*\\

(Japanese) A machine that plays a music video with the vocal track removed so that office workers can play at being rock stars on Friday nights. The word translates as "empty orchestra," not "off-key."

karate *kah-rah-tey*\\

(Japanese) A martial art form that famously involves black belts and doing hand-chops through wooden boards.

karma *kar-mah*\\

(Sanskrit) The concept in Hinduism and Buddhism that the sum of your actions in this life affects your future lives after reincarnation. (See page 121.)

karoshi *kah-roh-shee*\\

(Japanese) Death from overwork.

kasbah *kaz-bah*\

(Maghribi/Arabic) Also spelled *casbah*. A citadel in a North African city. (Also, something the 1980s rock band The Clash rocks.)

kawaii *kah-weye-ee*\

(Japanese) Ultra cute in a specifically Japanese way. Hello Kitty cute.

kayak *kay-yak*\

(Inuit) A hunting canoe covered with a skin to keep the water out.

kazachok *kah-zah-chok*\

(Ukrainian) This is the dance that Russian and Ukrainian people do where they squat and kick their legs out straight.

kef *kef*\

(Arabic) A state of drowsy good humor, especially as produced by smoking cannabis.

keiretsu *kee-ret-soo*\

(Japanese) A conglomeration of firms with related business interests.

keister *kee-ster*\

(Yiddish) A whimsical word for the buttocks.

KARMA VS. DHARMA

What is the difference between *karma* and *dharma*? In the Hindu and Buddhist conception, souls go through a cycle of birth and death known as reincarnation. Unlike in Christianity, where the ultimate reward for moral behavior is eternal life, in these Eastern religions, the ultimate goal of enlightenment is to escape the cycle of birth and death. In each lifetime, a person has a duty to behave in a manner that conforms with the guiding principles of the universe. This life duty is your *dharma*. How well you carry out this lifework determines your *karma*. *Karma* is the sum of your actions in life. If you have done more good than bad you will move on to a higher level upon rebirth, and *vice versa*.

We often use the word *karma* to refer to something much more immediate than a future life. In this sense, it means "you reap what you sow."

K

khan \kahn\
(Turkic) A central Asian ruler. Literally "lord, prince."

kibosh \keye-bosh\
(Yiddish) Used in the phrase "to put the *kibosh* on," meaning to squelch or stop something.

kimono \ki-moh-noh\
(Japanese) A long, loose, traditional Japanese robe. (My father used to use this word for "bathrobe.")

kindergarten \kin-der-gar-ten\
(German) "Children's garden." School for young children, a transition from preschool to a full day of schooling.

kismet \kiz-met\
(Turkish) Fate, destiny.

kitsch \kich\
(German) Tacky art objects that are appreciated ironically.

kiwi \kee-wee\
(Maori) A flightless bird native to New Zealand and by extension, a slang term for a New Zealander. In the U.S., there is also a "kiwi fruit," a fuzzy little green import. In New Zealand, they call it "Chinese gooseberry." It seems this name is more accurate as the fruit originally came from China.

klutz *kluts*\\
(Yiddish) A clumsy person.

knapsack *nap-sak*\\
(German) A backpack.

koan *koh-ahn*\\
(Japanese) In Zen Buddhism, a paradoxical statement or question often reflected on in meditation.

kosher *koh-sher*\\
(Yiddish from Hebrew) Food prepared according to Jewish dietary law.

kow tow *kow tow*\\
(Chinese) An old custom, no longer practiced, in which a person would kneel and touch his forehead to the ground as a sign of respect. This evolved into any act of obsequiousness or submission. "I am not going to *kow tow* to him!"

kudos *koo-dohs*\\
(Greek) High praise, congratulations.

kudzu *kud-zoo*\\
(Japanese) An invasive, East Asian, climbing plant introduced to the U.S. as an ornamental plant. It quickly became "the vine that ate the South."

K

kundalini \koon-dah-lee-nee\
(Sanskrit) A type of yoga meditation that channels the female energy believed to be coiled at the base of the spine.

kung fu \kung foo\
(Chinese) A martial art resembling *karate* and *judo*.

kvetch \kvech\
(Yiddish) To complain, or a person who enjoys complaining.

Kyrie eleison \kee-ree-ey ey-ley-ee-son\
(Greek) "Lord have mercy." An invocation used in the Anglican, Orthodox, and Roman Catholic churches.

labia majora \ley-bee-ah mah-jor-ah\
(Latin) "Great lips." An anatomical term for the outer fold of skin surrounding the vulva.

labia minora \ley-bee-ah meye nor-ah\
(Latin) "Lesser lips." An anatomical term for the inner folds of skin surrounding the vulva.

labor omnia vincit \ley-bor ohm-ee-ah vin-sit\
(Latin) "Labor conquers all." The state motto of Oklahoma.

laika \lay-kah\
(Russian) A Siberian breed of hunting dog. The name is derived from the Russian word "to bark," therefore "a barking dog." *Laika* is also a common Russian personal name for a dog, similar to the American "Spot" or "Rover." One of the first animals launched into space was a dog named Laika, sent into the cosmos (and to her death) on *Sputnik 2*.

laissez-faire \le-sey feyr\
(French) To leave it to do its thing. Usually applied to the economy.

lambada \lahm-bah-dah\
(Portuguese) A sexy Brazilian dance that had a brief surge of international popularity in the late 1980s.

lamé \lah-mey\
(French) A fabric made of shiny silver or gold metallic threads.

lamentoso \lah-men-toh-soh\
(Italian) Musical notation. To be played mournfully.

ländler \lant-ler\
(German) An Austrian dance similar to a slow waltz. (Maria and the Captain fall in love while dancing the ländler in the movie *The Sound of Music*.)

lapsus linguae \lap-sus ling-gwey\
(Latin) A slip of the tongue.

largess \lar-jes\
(French) Financial generosity. A usual context is "He bestows his *largess* upon . . ."

lassitude \lah-si-tood\
(French) Weariness. A state of sluggish exhaustion.

laureate \lor-ee-et\
(Latin) An honored person, especially in academia.

DOMO ARIGATO, MR. ROBOTO

In the 1980s, as business executives were studying Japanese business techniques, the MTV generation was enjoying a spate of linguistic pop-music borrowings.

There were German-language hit songs such as "Der Kommissar" (the Commissioner) by the Austrian pop star Falco and "99 Luftballons" ("99 Air Balloons," translated into "Red Balloons" in its English-language version) by the German group Nena. Falco's trademark was dropping foreign phrases into his German-language songs. "Der Kommissar" featured French *tout de suite* and English lines like "Babe, you know I miss my funky friends." There was even an odd song by an English punk band named Tenpole Tudor called "Wunderbar," which had a chorus consisting of the single word *wunderbar* repeated *ad nauseum* (but with great enthusiasm).

"Mr. Roboto," a hit song by Styx, made a chorus out of the Japanese phrase *domo arigato* or "thank you very much." Then there were the English bands who gave themselves foreign names. Depeche Mode is from a French magazine whose name translates to "fast fashion." Wang Chung's name means "yellow bell" in Chinese. What the lyric "Everybody *wang chung* tonight" means is anyone's guess.

L

lavage *lah-vahzh*\\
(French) A medical term for washing out a body cavity. A "stomach pump" in medicalese is a "gastric *lavage*."

lava-lava *lah-vah lah-vah*\\
(Samoan) Not the stuff that comes out of a volcano (twice). *Lava-lava* is a piece of printed cloth worn like a skirt by both men and women in Polynesia.

l'chaim or lechaim *lek-hay-em*\\
(Hebrew) "To life!" A toast. Popularized by a song in the musical *Fiddler on the Roof*.

lectio divina *lek-tee-oh di-veen-ah*\\
(Latin) "Divine reading." A system of prayer involving meditation on a passage of a sacred text.

lederhosen *ley-der-hoh-zen*\\
(German) "Leather trousers." A traditional Bavarian garment made up of leather shorts with H-shaped suspenders.

legato *le-gah-toh*\\
(Italian) Music played in a slow, smooth style.

legem pone *le-gem poh-ney*\\

(Latin) A now-obscure term for the payment of cash money, ready money. From the first words of Psalm 119. The psalm was read on the twenty-fifth day of each month. The first great payday of the year was March 25, and thus *legem pone* became associated with having cash to put down. The expression "pony up" may derive from *legem pone*.

leitmotif *layt moh-teef*\\

(German) A recurring musical theme associated with a particular character or emotion.

lexis *lek-sis*\\

(Greek) All of the words in a language.

liberté, égalité, fraternité

lee-ber-tey, ey-gahl-ee-tey, frah-ter-nee-tey\\
(French) "Liberty, equality, brotherhood" (or "fraternity") The rallying cry of the French Revolution.

libido *li-bee-doh*\\

(Latin) The motivating power of the sexual drive.

libretto *li-bre-toh*\\

(Italian) The text of an opera.

L

liebchen \leeb-shen\
(German) A term of affection: beloved, sweetheart.

lieu \loo\
(French) "Place." Usually used in the context "in *lieu* of." For example, "He used the French word for 'place' in *lieu* of the English."

lingua franca \ling-gwah fran-kah\
(Italian) A common language used by non-native speakers in order to communicate. The international language when the phrase was coined was French, thus, literally, "Frankish tongue."

literati \li-ter-ah-tee\
(Latin) A learned class of literature lovers.

loch \lok\
(Scots Gaelic) "Lake." The most famous *loch* is Loch Ness, known as the supposed home of a dragon-like monster.

loco \loh-koh\
(Spanish) Crazy.

loco citato \loh-koh see-tah-toh\
(Latin) "In the place cited." Used in bibliographic citation to refer to a previous mention of a particular word in the footnotes or endnotes.

locum tenens \loh-kum ten-enz\
(Latin) One who holds another's place.

locus classicus \loh-kus klas-i-kus\
(Latin) The most authoritative or best-known passage that one can use as an example from a standard work.

locus delicti \loh-kus dey-lik-tee\
(Latin) The scene of the crime.

loofah \loo-fah\
(Arabic) The dried, fibrous interior of a dishcloth gourd used as a rough sponge.

louche \loosh\
(French) Tacky; having bad taste. See also *gauche*.

luftmensch \looft-mench\
(Yiddish) A person with his head in the clouds, who has no practical plans for making a living.

luminarias \loo-mi-nar-ee-us\
(Spanish) Small paper bags with sand in the bottom containing votive candles that make the bags glow.

lusus naturae \loo-sus nah-tur-eye\
(Latin) A freak of nature.

macabre *mah-kah-bre*\

(French) Gruesome. Related to death.

macho *mah-choh*\

(Spanish) Manly. *Machismo* adds the suffix meaning "ism" to the adjective. It is *macho*-ism, the essential quality of *macho*-ness.

macramé *mak-rah-mey*\

(French) A decoration made by knotting chords. In the 1970s, it was a popular way to make holders for hanging plants.

madrasa *mah-drah-sah*\

(Arabic) A school for Islamic religious instruction.

maelstrom *meyl-strom*\

(Dutch) Literally, a whirlpool, but more often used to denote any turbulent and stormy experience.

maestro *meye-stroh*\

(Italian) A master musical conductor.

magna cum laude *mag-nah koom low-du*\

(Latin) An academic honorific that is above *cum laude* and below *summa cum laude*.

magnum opus *mag-num oh-pus*\

(Latin) An artist's most important work.

majolica *mah-jol-i-kah*\

(Italian) A bright and colorful glazed pottery originating on the island of Majolica. The island is now known as Majorca.

maladroit *mal-ah-droit*\

(French) Clumsy; awkward.

malamute *mal-ah-myoot*\

(Inupiaq) Inupiaq is an Inuit language spoken in Northern Alaska. A malamute is a type of sled dog bred by the Mahlemut people in this region.

mal de mer *mahl de mer*\

(French) Seasickness.

malgré lui *mahl-grey lwee*\

(French) A pompous way to say "in spite of himself."

mama mia *mah-mah mee-ah*\
(Italian) "My mother!" An exclamation of surprise. (See also *oy vey*, *uff da*, and page 211).

mambo *mahm-boh*\
(Spanish) A Latin American ballroom dance.

mañana *mahn-yah-nah*\
(Spanish) "Tomorrow." That magical time when you will take care of all the things you'd rather put off. "The sink needs to be fixed? *Mañana.*"

mandala *mahn-dah-lah*\
(Sanskrit) A circular design representing the universe, often created or contemplated as an aid to meditation.

manga *mahn-gah*\
(Japanese) In Japan, it just means "comic book." Americans use it specifically to refer to Japanese comics.

mano a mano *mah-noh ah mah-noh*\
(Spanish) English speakers often assume this means "man to man." It literally means "hand to hand" in the sense of one-on-one combat.

ma non troppo *mah nohn troh-poh*\
(Italian) "But not too much."

mantra *mahn-trah*\\

(Sanskrit) In meditation, a word repeated to aid in concentration. Conversationally, it has come to mean a personal slogan or aphorism, something the speaker often repeats. "Never argue over stupid stuff, that's my *mantra*."

maracas *mah-rah-kahz*\\

(Portugese) Hand shakers made from hollowed-out gourds filled with beans or pebbles. Although there is a singular—*maraca*—the instruments are usually used in pairs.

Mardi Gras *mahr-dee grah*\\

(French) "Fat Tuesday." A celebration of feasting and reveling before the austere season of Lent.

mariachi *mar-ee-ah-chee*\\

(Spanish) A small musical group that plays traditional Mexican music.

marijuana *mar-i-wah-nah*\\

(Spanish) Were Mary and Jane stoners? They must have been, because the Spanish word for the medicinal and recreational weed derives from the names "Mary" and "Jane" in Spanish.

marimba *mah-rim-bah*\\

(Bantu) A xylophone-like percussion instrument originating in Mali.

WEED

When something is illegal or taboo, all sorts of euphemistic ways are invented to talk about it. This is certainly true of the psychoactive parts of the hemp plant. *Cannabis* is the name of the plant genus. The word is Latin but derives ultimately from the Greek *kannabis* which simply means "hemp." (The word "canvas" incidentally derives from the same root and originally meant hemp fabric.) If you type "slang terms for marijuana" into your favorite search engine, you will find pages and pages of creative terminology. There is the West Indian *spliff*, the Afrikaans *dagga* and the Arabic *hashish* for powdered hemp. Right now, we'll turn our focus to just two options in a crowded field.

MARIJUANA

By far, the most common word for the drug came to us from Mexico. Ultimately the word *marijuana* seems to derive from the personal names "Mary" and "Jane," but no one knows why.

GANJA

Although the word *ganja* (sometimes spelled *ganjah*) comes from India, it is most associated with the Caribbean—especially Jamaica, where it is a fixture in reggae songs. (I personally recommend "Ganja Smuggling" by Eek-a-Mouse.)

THE WINNER?

Hindi. Until the Mexicans can tell us who Mary and Jane are, India takes it. So head out to a reggae festival, mon.

matador *mat-ah-dor*\
(Spanish) A professional bullfighter. The word literally means "bull killer."

materia medica *mah-tee-ree-ah med-i-kah*\
(Latin) "The stuff of medicine." A largely archaic term for the body of knowledge about the properties of drugs, now referred to as "pharmacology."

matryoshka *mah-tree-yosh-kah*\
(Russian) Wooden nesting dolls.

mauvais quart d'heure *moh-vey kahr der*\
(French) "A bad fifteen minutes." That is to say, a difficult, but short-lived experience.

mazel tov *mah-zel tof*\
(Yiddish) Congratulations. "You've made it all the way to letter M. Mazel tov!"

mazurka *mah-zur-kah*\
(Polish) A traditional folk dance similar to the polka.

mea culpa *mey-ah kul-pah*\
(Latin) An admission of guilt or self-blame, an apology. Example: "The politician's wife stood beside him as he gave his mea culpa."

megillah \mu-gi-lah\
(Yiddish) A slang term for a long, involved, and usually dull story. Generally used in the expression "the whole megillah." Derived from the Hebrew word for "scroll," it is a reference to the megillah of Esther, which is read twice during the festival of Purim.

mêlée \mey-ley\
(French) A battle or brawl. Usually spelled without the accent marks in English.

mele Kalikimaka \me-le kah-lee-kee-mah-kah\
(Hawaiian) The Hawaiian phrase made famous by the Bing Crosby song is not a native phrase. It is, rather, how the Hawaiians heard the English "Merry Christmas." We borrowed their version back.

ménage à trois \me-nazh ah twah\
(French) A romantic or sexual relationship between three people.

mensch \mensh\
(Yiddish) A good guy.

mens rea \menz ree-ah\
(Latin) Criminal intent.

LE MENU

Because we use so many French terms for restaurant meals, you probably think you could go to France and order from a menu with little confusion, *n'est ce pas*? *Au contraire*. Were life only that simple. We use French words in our restaurants, but we do not use them the way the French do.

Let's begin with the word *menu* itself. In France the term *le menu* refers to a style of dining where you pay a fixed price for an entire meal consisting of a number of courses selected by the *chef*. What we call a "menu" is what the French call *la carte*, a list of food choices with individual prices that the diner can select to make up his own courses. So when we say *á la carte*, meaning "individually priced," we're literally saying "off the menu."

We use the word *entrée* to mean the main dish. In French this means an "entrance" and refers to an opening to the meal, synonymous with *hors d'oeuvre*. We use the word *hors d'oeuvre* ("outside of the *oeuvre*" or main work) also. In English, it is synonymous with "appetizer." If you want to say "main dish" in French, you say "*le plat principal.*"

merengue *mer-en-gey*\
(Spanish) The traditional dance form of the Dominican Republic, also popular in neighboring Puerto Rico. The name implies that the dance is a confection because it is derived from the sweet dessert "meringue," but no one quite knows why.

mesa *mey-sah*\
(Spanish) A land formation like a hill with a flat top. A mesa is like a plateau, but smaller.

meshuga *me-shug-ah*\
(Yiddish from Hebrew) Crazy or stupid. From an expression meaning "to wander away." (See page 193.)

mezzanine *mez-ah-neen*\
(French) An intermediate balcony in a theater, or story in a building.

miasma *mee-az-mah*\
(Greek) A foul, noxious vapor, like fumes rising from a swamp. Also, an emotionally unhealthy or corrupting atmosphere.

mi casa es su casa *mee kah-sah es soo kah-sah*\
(Spanish) "My house is your house."

VIPs AND CHINOOK SPELLED BADLY

When European settlers came into contact with the native peoples of the North American continent, they sometimes borrowed words from their languages. Often they had no idea how to spell, or quite how to pronounce, them. Such a word is "mucky-muck," an American slang term for a wealthy big shot. A "mucky-muck" is the type of person who lights cigars with one-hunded-dollar bills while wearing a tuxedo. *Muckamuck* was the Chinook tribe's word for "food." It implied a diet rich in whale meat. In fact, early settlers in the Northwest used to use the word *muckamuck* as a verb meaning "to eat," but its usage evolved to embrace the colonial truth that a well-fed person was an important person.

mise en place *meez ahn plahs*\\
(French) Preparing of food and ingredients before meal service in a restaurant.

mise en scène *meez ahn sen*\
(French) The physical setting. The visual composition of actors and scenery in a theatrical production or film.

mitzvah *mits-vah*\
(Hebrew) A good deed done as a form of religious devotion.

moccasin *mok-ah-sin*\
(Algonquin) A soft leather shoe without a heel.

modus operandi *moh-dus o-per-an-day*\
(Latin) A way of doing something.

monstre sacré *mon-stre sahk-rey*\
(French) A "sacred monster." An obscure term that deserves to be resurrected. It refers to a celebrity who is scandalous and outrageous in a strangely irresistible way. A horrifying and fascinating public figure we love to hate.

mons veneris *monz ve-ne-ris*\
(Latin) "Hill of Venus." The rounded covering of the female pubic arch.

montani semper liberi
    mon-tah-nee sem-per lee-ber-ee\
(Latin) "Mountaineers are always free." The state motto of West Virginia.

morgue *morg*\\
(French) Originally, the Morgue was a proper name of a specific building in Paris where relatives of the missing could come and view the dead bodies of those drowned in the Seine. The word did not enter English until 1821. Prior to that, such places were called "dead houses."

morituri te salutant *mor-ee-tur-ee tey sal-yoo-tahnt*\\
(Latin) "Those who are about to die salute you." This, after *Ave Caesar* or "Hail Caesar" was the salute the gladiators gave when entering the arena.

mortuum flagellas *mor-too-um flah-gel-ahs*\\
(Latin) "Beating the dead." How someone with a lot of classical education says "beating a dead horse."

(le) mot juste *moh zhoost*\\
(French) "(The) right word."

mujahadin or **mujahadeen** *moo-jah-he-deen*\\
(Persian) Muslim guerrilla fighters in the Middle East. Literally people who practice *jihad*.

mukluk *muk-luk*\\
(Inuit) A boot made of reindeer or seal skin, lined with soft fur.

mullah *mu-lah*\
(Turkish) A person who is highly knowledgeable in Islamic law.

münsterlander *moon-ster-lan-der*\
(German) A breed of hunting dog from Münster, Germany.

mustachio *mus-ta-shee-oh*\
(Spanish) Mustache. Usually used to describe a particularly impressive example of the fashion with a bit of comic effect. Also used in the form: "a *mustachio*ed gentleman."

muumuu *moo-moo*\
(Indigenous Hawaiian) A long, loose, formless dress.

nabob *ney-bob*\\

(Hindi) Originally a deputy governor, it evolved into a general term for a man of wealth and power, especially someone who is seen to have too much wealth and power. One of the most famous uses of the word was spoken by Spiro Agnew (written by his speechwriter William Safire) to refer to the press: "nattering *nabobs* of negativism."

nacelle *nah-sel*\\

(French) A bulge on the fuselage housing an engine, especially on an airplane wing.

naches *nahk-hes*\\

(Yiddish) Gratification and pride, especially at the achievements of one's children.

nada *nah-dah*\\

(Spanish) "Nothing."

nag champa *nahg shahm-pah*\\

(Sanskrit) An Indian fragrance, especially popular with hippies. It is primarily used in incense but also soap and essential oils. The name is derived from the champa flower,

To the Russians!
NA ZDAROVYE!
\nuh zdah-rohv-ee\

If you only know one Russian expression, it is probably this one. But when you raise a glass to a real Russian to give the famous toast *na zdarovye* ("to your health") he or she will look at you a bit sideways. It is a Russian phrase, and technically could be used for a toast, but generally isn't. A real Russian is more likely to say is "*za vashe* [or *tvoyo* if familiar] *zdarovye*" or "to your health." A simpler Russian toast is *za vas*, "to you" ("you" here is formal and/or plural), or *za nas*, "to us." Real Russians, however, are fond of personal, complimentary, emotional toasts that go on for upward of a minute. These grow longer as the night wears on. The toast should be elaborate. The drink should not: always drink the vodka straight.

also known as the plumeria, and *nag* meaning "breath" or "spirit." Therefore *nag champa* means "the breath or spirit of the champa flower."

naïve *neye-eev*\\
(French) Innocent, unworldly, easily fooled. *Naïveté* is the quality of being *naïve*.

namaste *nah-mah-stey*\\
(Sanskrit) "I bow to you." A respectful Hindu greeting.

nebbish *neb-ish*\\
(Yiddish) A timid, weak person.

née *ney*\\
(French) "Born," in reference to a woman's maiden name. "Hillary Clinton, *née* Rodham."

negligee *neg-li-zhey*\\
(French) A lightweight night gown. The name is derived from the verb "to neglect." Coined in the mid-1700s, it meant something a woman threw on without care, compared to the elaborate hoop skirts, boned bodices, and powdered wigs she wore in public.

nemesis *ne-mi-sis*\\
(Greek) A formidable enemy, derived from the name of an ancient goddess of divine retribution.

nenju *nen-joo*\\
(Japanese) Buddhist prayer beads. From *nen* for "mindful thinking" and *ju* for "beads."

ne plus ultra *ney plus ool-trah*\\
(Latin) The apex. No higher to climb.

n'est-ce pas? *ncs pah*\\
(French) "Isn't it?" Sometimes used for Frenchy effect when you expect someone to agree with what you just said. "The weather is lovely today, *n'est-ce pas?*"

niche *neesh*\\
(French) A trough or groove, or more metaphorically, the place a person fits as though slotted into such a space. In marketing, it refers to a particular demand that one's products or services can fill. "A *niche* market."

nil desperandum *nil des-per-ahn-dum*\\
(Latin) "Never despair."

ninja *nin-jah*\\
(Japanese) A samurai who was an expert in the martial art form known as *ninjutsu*. Ninjas were not well known outside of Japan until they became characters in computer and role-playing games in the late 1970s and early 1980s.

N

niqab *ni-kahb*\\
(Arabic) A veil for the face that leaves only the area around the eyes open. Worn by Muslim women with an accompanying headscarf.

nirvana *ner-vah-nah*\\
(Sanskrit) In Buddhism, the end of repeated cycles of birth and death and the final abandonment of the ego. (Also a 1990s rock band.)

noblesse oblige *noh-bles oh-bleezh*\\
(French) The idea that being a member of the aristocracy comes with a responsibility to help those who are worse off.

nocturne *nahk-turn*\\
(French) A piece of slow, sad music appropriate for the night.

Noël *noh-el*\\
(French) Christmas.

noh *noh*\\
(Japanese) A highly stylized theatrical form consisting of short tragedies filled with poetry and dance, but minimal plot.

nolle prosequi *no-ley pro-sek-wee*\\
(Latin) A legal term that means "we shall no longer prosecute." It is used when the case against a defendant is dropped.

nolo contendere *noh-loh kon-ten-de-rey*\\
(Latin) "I do not wish to contend." In court, a term used to describe a defendant who has decided neither to admit nor contest the charges.

nom de guerre *nahm de ger*\\
(French) "War name." An *alias* under which someone goes to battle.

nom de plume *nahm de ploom*\\
(French) "Pen name." (See page 152.)

non bis in idem *nohn bis in i-dem*\\
(Latin) "Not twice for the same thing." A legal term prohibiting double jeopardy.

non compos mentis *non kom-pohs men-tis*\\
(Latin) A legal term for a person who is not in his right mind.

non sequitur *non sek-wi-tur*\\
(Latin) "It does not follow." A statement that is bizarrely unrelated to what came before it.

nostalgie de la boue *noh-stahl-zhee de lah boo*\\
(French) "Mud nostalgia." When someone who has risen out of poverty looks back at his humble beginnings with a wistful longing to return.

MOCK FRENCH
C'EST WHAT?

Nom de plume is a phrase in French, but it is not a French phrase. It was adopted by nineteenth-century English poets as a riff on the expression the French actually use for "pseudonym": *nom de guerre*, which translates literally to "name of war" and came from French soldiers giving fake names when they enlisted.

nota bene *no-tah be-ney*\\
(Latin) "Note well." It is used in writing to call attention to something significant.

nouveau riche *noo-voh reesh*\\
(French) A newly wealthy individual. Often with the sense that the person is showy about money and not as classy as old-monied families.

nouvelle vague \noo-vel vahg\
(French) "New wave." Refers to a late-1950s cinema style originating in France.

nuance \noo-ahns\
(French) A subtle shade of difference. The word is similar to the French word for "cloud" and some etymologists argue that its origin is a reference to the different shades of color in the clouds. If it is not, it really ought to be.

nudnik \nood-nik\
(Yiddish) A tedious, boring person who will not go away.

numero uno \noo-mer-oh oo-noh\
(Italian) Also Spanish, but with an accent mark: *número uno*. Number one. The best. The head *honcho*.

nunchaku \nun-chah-koo\
(Japanese) Two hardwood sticks joined together by a chain and used as a martial arts weapon. Often anglicized to "nunchucks."

obbligato \ah-blee-gah-toh\
(Italian) Something that is necessary and not to be omitted.
In music, it's used to refer to an instrumental part that is an
integral part of the composition.

obiter dictum \oh-bi-ter dik-tum\
(Latin) A judge's incidental remark. (The plural is *obiter dicta*.)

objet d'art \ob-zhey dar\
(French) A work of art.

obscurum per obscurius
\ob-skyoo-rahm per ob-skyoo-ree-us\
(Latin) Explaining something obscure by means of something
even more obscure. A term used in logic.

octavo \ok-tey-voh\
(Latin) Printers' terminology for sheets folded to make eight
leaves.

odalisque \oh-dahl-isk\
(Turkish) A female slave or concubine, sometimes used to refer
to any attractive woman.

odium \oh-dee-um\
(Latin) Hatred; repugnance.

oeuvre \oo-vruh\
(French) The body of work a writer, composer, or artist creates
over his or her entire lifetime.

olé \oh-ley\
(Spanish) *Olé* is Spanish for *bravo.* (See page 157.)

om \ohm or owm\
(Sanskrit) A sacred symbol representing the three major gods
of Hinduism; used in meditation to focus concentration.

ombré \ahm-brey\
(French) With colors blending into one another from light
shades to dark.

omnia vincit amor \ohm-nee-ah vin-sit ah-mor\
(Latin) "Love conquers all."

omnibus \ahm-ni-bus\
(Latin) An edition of a book which brings all of the past stories
together in one volume. Also, a piece of legislation that
packages many earlier bills together into one.

onus \oh-nus\
(Latin) Burden. "She put the *onus* on him to finish the long-overdue report on *tchotchke* imports." *Onus probandi* is the legal term for "burden of proof."

opa! \oh-pah\
(Greek) This Greek exclamation is difficult to translate. It is often heard at restaurants when cheese is set on fire or when a plate is broken, or is shouted as the Greek version of *bravo* when watching impressive dancing. The best translation might be "Hey!"

ora pro nobis \oh-rah proh noh-bees\
(Latin) "Pray for us."

oratorio \or-ah-tor-ee-oh\
(Italian) A musical composition that dramatizes a religious story.

origami \or-i-gahm-ee\
(Japanese) The Japanese art of paper folding.

orihon \or-ee-hon\
(Japanese) A book made out of a manuscript folded accordion-style.

oro y plata \or-oh ee plah-tah\
(Spanish) "Gold and silver." The state motto of Montana.

ORIGIN OF OLÉ

Name a word of foreign origin that is an exclamation of wonder at transcendent beauty. Did *olé* come to mind? Probably not. Today, it is associated most strongly with bull fighting, but in fact, *olé* derives ultimately from the Arabic word for god, "Allah."

It goes back to the days when North African Moors ruled the Iberian peninsula. While they were there, they loaned a lot of words to the people of what is now Spain. It is estimated that four thousand words, about 8 percent of the Spanish lexicon, come directly from Arabic.

The Moors believed that artistic expression, such as beautiful dancing, was channeled through the artist directly from god. Whenever a dancer moved with transcendent grace, members of the audience would spontaneously shout "Allah!" The balletic movements of the bull ring also warranted such a "*bravo*." Non-Moorish residents misheard this, and it evolved into *olé* and eventually lost its connection with Allah.

O

otaku *oh-tah-koo*\\

(Japanese) An obsessive fan of something, usually some kind of *manga* or *anime*. It literally means "your house" and paints a picture of a person who is so obsessed with a hobby that he or she never goes outside.

oubliette *oo-blee-et*\\

(French) This word for a dungeon with a trapdoor has largely fallen out of use because we encounter so few of them these days. It derives from the French word meaning "to forget" and it implies a prison to which you banish people you wish to put out of your mind forever. This is an idea that seems ripe to be brought back in a more metaphorical sense.

outré *oo-trey*\\

(French) Out there, bizarre, eccentric.

oyez! oyez! oyez! *oi-yey* etc.\\

(French) French for "Hear ye! Hear ye! Hear ye!"

oy vey *oy vey*\\

(Yiddish) An interjection of exasperation. Sometimes a simple *oy* will do. (See page 211.)

pachinko *pah-ching-koh*\
(Japanese) A vertical pinball machine.

padre *pah-drey*\
(Spanish) A priest.

palomino *pal-oh-mee-noh*\
(Spanish) A tan horse with a white mane and tail.

panacea *pan-ah-see-ah*\
(Greek) A cure-all. From the name of one of the daughters of
the Greek god of healing.

panache *pah-nash*\
(French) A bold, stylish manner. (See page 39.)

papier-mâché *pah-pee-yey mah-shey*\
(French) Pulped paper mixed with glue and then molded.

papoose *pah-poos*\
(Narragansett) An American-Indian child, though this usage
is considered offensive. Now, a type of bag used to carry a
child on one's back.

paramour *pah-rah-moor*\
(French) A lover or mistress.

par excellence *par ek-sel-ahns*\
(French) Better than others in its class.

pariah *pah-ray-yah*\
(Tamil) A social outcast, from the name of a member of a low caste in India.

pari-mutuel *pe-re myoo-choo-el*\
(French) A betting pool.

parthenogenesis *par-the-noh-jen-e-sis*\
(Greek) A form of reproduction in which an unfertilized egg develops.

particeps criminis *pahr-ti-seps kri-mi-nis*\
(Latin) A partner in crime, an accomplice.

pas de deux *pah de du*\
(French) A duet in ballet.

paso doble *pah-soh doh-bley*\
(Spanish) A "double step" is a brisk Latin American ballroom dance.

passe-partout \pahs par-too\
(French) "Pass everywhere." Used to refer to a universal passkey.

pastiche \pas-teesh\
(French) A medley made up of fragments from different works.

patchouli \pah-choo-lee\
(Tamil) An aromatic oil made from an Indian plant from the mint family, worn as a perfume by hippies and artsy counter-cultural types.

paterfamilias \pah-ter fah-mee-lee-us\
(Latin) The father of the family, the male head of the household.

patois \pah-twah\
(French) A regional dialect. Often used for a dialect considered to be rustic and lower class.

Pax Romana \paks roh-mah-nah\
(Latin) "Roman peace." It was a peace that was maintained by the threat that enemies of the empire would be crushed.

pax vobiscum \paks voh-bis-kahm\
(Latin) "Peace be with you." The "you" is plural. Part of the traditional Roman Catholic mass.

peccadillo *pek-ah-di-loh*\
(Spanish) A "little sin." A minor offense.

pendente lite *pen-den-tee li-tee*\
(Latin) While a lawsuit is pending. "*Pendente lite* my lawyer advises me not to call you a *roué* and a cur."

peon *pee-yon*\
(Portuguese) A low-ranking person, someone from the lowest rung of society. An unskilled worker who must take any job he or she can get. More generally, the guy at the office who has to do all the stuff no one else wants to do.

per annum *per ah-noom*\
(Latin) "Per year."

per capita *per kap-i-tah*\
(Latin) "According to heads." Per person, rather than considering the members of a society as a group.

per diem *per dee-em*\
(Latin) A fee paid each day to cover expenses.

per se *per sey*\
(Latin) As such.

THOSE FUNNY COLONIALISTS

PECCAVI \pey-kah-vee\

An anecdote from 1843, the truth of which is highly debatable, says that the British general Sir Charles Napier took Miani in central Sindh, India, in a military campaign. Apparently a clever word player and a minor scholar in Latin, he wrote a one-word message to his superiors to announce his conquest. "*Peccavi*," it said. "I have sinned." A *double entendre* for colonialism if ever there was one.

persona non grata \per-soh-nah non grah-tah\
(Latin) An unwelcome person.

petit mal \pe-tee mahl\
(French) "Little sickness." Petit mal seizures are also known as "absence seizures." They involve brief sudden lapses of consciousness in which the victim appears to be staring into space. (See also *grand mal*.)

pharynx *far-inks*\\
(Greek) Medical term for the windpipe. From the Greek word for "throat."

pianissimo *pee-ahn-is-i-moh*\\
(Italian) Music played softly.

pibroch *pee-brok*\\
(Scots Gaelic) A piece of martial music with a series of variations on a theme played on the bagpipes.

piñata *pin-yah-tah*\\
(Spanish) A *papier-mâché* figure, often in the form of an animal, which is filled with small toys or candy and suspended so that blindfolded children can whack at it with a stick until it unleashes its bounty (at which point, the kid who actually broke it open finds himself scrambling with the non-blindfolded kids who get to all the treasures first).

pirouette *pir-oo-et*\\
(French) To turn or spin, especially in ballet.

pis-aller *pee zah-ley*\\
(French) The worst that can happen.

pissoir *pee-swahr*\\
(French) A public urinal.

pizzicato *pit-sah-kah-toh*\\
(Italian) Plucking the strings of an instrument, such as a violin, with one's fingers rather than playing with a bow.

placebo *plah-see-boh*\\
(Latin) A medicine made of inert material given for psychological effect. *Placebo* is the first-person future tense of the Latin *placere* and literally means "I will please."

plat du jour *plah doo zhoor*\\
(French) In an upscale restaurant, the daily special.

plein-air *plen er*\\
(French) Literally "in full air," it refers to a style of painting of outdoor scenes popular in the nineteenth century.

plié *plee-yey*\\
(French) To bend. Used in ballet to indicate bending the knees and lowering the body.

plotz *plots*\\
(Yiddish) To fall over from shock, tiredness, or extreme emotion.

plus ça change, plus c'est la même chose
  ploo sah shahnzh ploo sey lah mem shohz\\
(French) "The more things change, the more they are the same." Often shortened to *plus ça change*.

pogrom *pah-grom*\

(Russian) "Devastation." The organized killing of a population based on their ethnic or religious identity. Usually refers to the historic massacres of Russian Jews in the nineteenth and early-twentieth centuries.

point d'appui *pwahn da-pwee*\

(French) A fortified point anchoring an army's position.

poltergeist *pol-ter-gayst*\

(German) "A noisy ghost." A ghost that makes noises and moves things around the house.

Pontifex Maximus *pon-ti-feks mak-si-mus*\

(Latin) The title of the pope.

portico *port-i-koh*\

(Italian) An open-roofed space held up by columns at the entrance to a building.

portmanteau *port-man-toh*\

(French) A traveling case with many compartments. (See the next page.)

THE EGG CAME FIRST

From the French word meaning "a piece of luggage with separate compartments" comes a linguistic term for a word that combines the sounds of two existing words to make a new combined word—a *portmanteau* word." The supreme example is breakfast + lunch = brunch.

I'm guessing you did not know that this term traces its origins to Humpty Dumpty. This is true. According to the *Oxford English Dictionary*, the first use of *portmanteau* for a lexical mashup was in Lewis Carroll's *Through the Looking Glass*, in which Humpty explains the meaning of the poem "The Jabberwocky" to Alice: "Well, 'slithy' means 'lithe and slimy.' 'Lithe' is the same as 'active.' You see it's like a portmanteau—there are two meanings packed up into one word." Even the Jabberwock itself was a *portmaneau*, with "jabber" blending into *wocor*, an Anglo-Saxon word for "offspring" or "fruit."

Lewis Carroll loved him some *portmunteaus*. Some of his most enduring coinages are "chortle" a combination of "chuckle" and "snort," and "galumph," which combines "gallop" and "triumph." He was far ahead of his time, considering modern English is full of "bromances," "ginormous" numbers, and lots of "chillaxing."

post hoc ergo propter hoc
post hok er-goh prop-ter hok\
(Latin) "After the thing therefore because of the thing." Refers to the logical fallacy that because one thing happened after another, the first thing must have caused the second to happen.

post meridiem *post me-ri-dee-em*\
(Latin) "After noon." This is what P.M. stands for.

post partum *post par-tum*\
(Latin) After the birth of a baby.

post scriptum *post skrip-tum*\
(Latin) "Written after." This is what P.S. stands for.

prêt à porter *pret ah por-tey*\
(French) A fashion term for "ready to wear" or off-the-rack clothes. That is, the kind most of us wear these days, as opposed to clothing made to order.

prima ballerina absoluta
pree-mah ba-ler-ee-nah ab-soh-loo-tah\
(Italian) The ultimate, number-one ballerina in a company.

prima facie *pree-mah fey-shee*\
(Latin) "On its face." In law, a case in which it appears that there is enough evidence to proceed.

primum non nocere *pree mum non noh-se-rey*\\
(Latin) "First do no harm." A medical maxim from the first line of the physician's Hippocratic Oath.

prix fixe *prec feeks*\\
(French) A restaurant meal with fixed courses and prices, as contrasted with an *à la carte* menu. The French use the word *menu* when a restaurant serves a set course, and in French *la carte* is what we call generally "the menu," a list of items you can order individually. Got it? (If not, see page 140.)

pro bono *proh boh-noh*\\
(Latin) "For the good," as opposed to "for the money."

pro forma *proh for-mah*\\
(Latin) A formality.

protégé *proh-tey-zhey*\\
(French) A person being tutored and mentored.

pro tempore *proh tem-por*\\
(Latin) Temporarily. Often abbreviated *pro tem*.

provenance *proh-ve-nahns*\\
(French) The origin or history, especially of an antique or work of art.

proviso *proh-vee-zoh*\
(Latin) A clause in a legal document that details a particular condition or limitation.

proxime accessit *proks-ee-mey ak-ses-it*\
(Latin) The runner-up. Someone who is almost, but not quite, a winner.

putsch *putch*\
(German) A revolution or coup.

al Qaeda \al kay-dah\

(Arabic) Because Arabic uses a different alphabet, this name, meaning "the base," has a number of English spellings. The name was coined by the U.S. government, not the terrorist organization itself, and spread by the media. Originally the group surrounding Osama bin Laden was known as *Al Jamaat al Sheikh* or "the Sheikh's group." *Al-Qaeda* originally referred specifically to the military base where they trained.

qi \chee\

(Chinese) Vital energy which flows around the body and in the environment. (Also spelled *chi* and a common crossword puzzle word. See page 174.)

qigong \chee-gong\

(Chinese) A spiritual practice, usually involving meditation and physical movement, that cultivates the proper flow of *qi*.

quandong tree \kwahn-dong tree\

(Indigenous Australian) A sandalwood tree with edible berries.

Q

quasi \kwah-zee\
(Latin) Resembling. A bit like. Almost.

quatrain \kwah-treyn\
(French) In poetry, a stanza of four lines.

quetzal \ket-sahl\
(Spanish) A brightly colored bird that lives in the mountains of
Central America.

quid pro quo \kwid proh kwoh\
(Latin) Tit for tat. You scratch my back, and I'll scratch yours.

quietus \kweye-ee-tus\
(Latin) Originally, the term referred to the discharge of a
financial account, but it evolved to mean the discharge of life
as in Hamlet's "To Be or Not to Be" speech.

quinzee \kwin-zee\
(Ojibwa) An igloo-like, round snow shelter.

qui tacet consentit \kwee tah-ket kahn-sen-tit\
(Latin) "He who remains silent consents."

quod erat demonstrandum
    \kwohd e-raht de-mon-strahn-dum\
(Latin) "Thus it is demonstrated." Usually abbreviated Q.E.D.

MOCK SPANISH
(OR ITALIAN? OR FRENCH?)
QUE SERA SERA

The expression *que sera sera*, as popularized by a 1950s Doris Day song, translates as "whatever will be will be." But what language does it translate from? Sometimes the phrase is spelled *che sera sera*, which renders it a bit more mock-Italian than mock-Spanish. It is not grammatically correct in either. What is more, there is no evidence that this was ever a proverb that was used in Italy or Spain. It is in any case very old, dating back to a Frenchy variant in the fifteenth century, *quy serra serra*. *Qui sera sera* would be bad modern French. Lee Hartman, a scholar who has studied the issue, posits that it is "conceivably permissible in Old and Middle French," but for various reasons, he doubts the hypothesis. In any case, there is no evidence that the French ever used *que sera sera*. So it appears to be an ancient mistranslation of an English thought into one of these European languages. Will we ever have the answer? *Que sera sera*.

CHINESE VS. FRENCH
THE ENERGY OF LIFE

QI

This is the vital life force or energy that flows through all living beings. It is the basis of a variety of Chinese practices in alternative medicine, martial arts, and interior design (*feng shui*).

ÉLAN VITAL

The expression *élan vital* was coined by French philosopher Henri Bergson to describe the impetus that drove evolution, the same mystical spark acted on consciousness.

THE WINNER?

The Chinese and French mystical life energies could arguably be referring to the same thing. In any case, parsing the subtle distinctions in the philosophies that these words come from is well beyond the scope of this book. Let's call this one a tie.

quod vide _kwahd vee-dey_\\
(Latin) "Which see." Abbreviated _q.v._

quoll _kwol_\\
(Guugu Yimidhirr, Indigenous Australian) A catlike, spotted marsupial native to Australia.

quo vadis _kwoh vah-dis_\\
(Latin) "Where are you going?" It is the question that Peter asked Jesus, and in turn, Jesus' reply gave Peter the courage to be martyred.

raconteur \ra-kon-tur\
(French) An entertaining storyteller. "Oscar Wilde was a
raconteur par excellence."

raison d'être \rey-zon de-tre\
(French) "Reason for being." One's life purpose.

rajah \rah-jah\
(Hindi) A Hindu prince.

ranchero \ran-cher-oh\
(Spanish) A rancher.

rapport \ra-por\
(French) Getting along well with another person.

rapprochement \rah-prohch-mon\
(French) Making peace, re-establishing relations.

rara avis \re-rah ey-vis\
(Latin) "Strange bird." A unique and perhaps eccentric
person, but unlike our expression "odd duck," it has a positive
connotation. This rare bird is strange in an admirable way.

MOCK LATIN
REDUCTIO AD HITLERUM

This useful term was coined by German-American philosopher Leo Strauss. *Reductio ad* is real Latin for "reduction to," paired with a Latinization of the name Hitler. It refers to the intellectual fallacy (especially common on the Internet) of dragging Hitler into your argument. "You know who else was in favor of [whatever you disagree with] . . . Hitler!"

rathskeller *rath-skel-er*\
(German) A basement beer hall.

rattenuto *rah-ten-oo-toh*\
(Italian) An instruction to perform a musical passage in a restrained manner.

réchauffé *rey-show-fey*\
(French) "Reheated." Something you do with leftover food or stale ideas.

recto *rek-toh*\
(Latin) The right-hand page of a book.

regnat populus *reg-naht pop-yoo-lus*\
(Latin) "The people rule." The state motto of Arkansas.

reiki *rey-kee*\
(Japanese) An alternative-medicine practice involving the laying on of hands to balance universal life energy.

remouillage *re-moo-yahzh*\
(French) "Rewetting." In culinary terms, it is using bones a second time for stock.

rendez-vous or **rendezvous** *rahn-dey-voo*\
(French) In French, a *rendez-vous* is a meeting. Because of stereotypes about the French, the term has connotations in English of a secret meeting with a *paramour*. Ooh là là!

repartee *re-pahr-tee*\
(French) A clever conversation full of witty replies and *bon mots*.

répondez s'il vous plaît
    rey-pon-dey seel voo pley\
(French) "Please reply." It's what you're saying when you write the abbreviation R.S.V.P.

À la Recherche de l'Emploi Perdu
"IN SEARCH OF LOST WORK"

When English speakers go job hunting, we carry pieces of paper with our employment history printed on them (or at least that's what we did before we started e-mailing and uploading). Job hunters in the U.S. and the U.K. each use foreign words for these documents. Curiously, we use different foreign words on each side of the ocean.

In the U.S., you're most likely to refer to your *résumé*, the French word for "summary."

In the U.K., it's a *c.v.*, a short version of the Latin *curriculum vitae*, which translates to the much more poetic "the course of one's life." It is essentially a *résumé* in most countries, but if an American employer asks for one, they usually want a fairly lengthy and comprehensive biography, which is yet another thing for hungry workers-to-be to spell-check.

R

requiem \re-kwee-em\
(Italian) A musical composition written to honor the dead.

requiescat in pace \re-kwee-e-skaht in pah-chey\
(Latin) "Rest in peace." The source of the abbreviation R.I.P., which works equally well as an abbreviation for its English equivalent.

res gestae \rez jes-tey\
(Latin) The events or circumstances surrounding a particular legal case.

residuum \re-zid-yoo-um\
(Latin) The residue or remainder. What is left over.

res inter alios \rez in-ter al-ee-ohs\
(Latin) "A matter between others." Something beyond the scope of the current issue (usually litigation).

res ipsa loquitur \rez ip-sah loh-kwi-tur\
(Latin) The fact that there is an injury implies negligence in itself.

ricercare \ree-cher-kah-rey\
(Italian) A complex prelude written for the lute or keyboard.

rigor mortis \ri-gor mor-tis\
(Latin) Stiffening of the muscles after death.

riposte \ri-pohst\
(French) Originally a fencing term referring to a quick thrust
after parrying an attack. It has come to mean a quick verbal
response as well, a retort.

risqué \risk-ey\
(French) Literally "risky," but we use the word to refer to things
that are just on the edge of being salacious and saucy,
loaded with *innuendo*.

ritenuto \ree-ten-oo-toh\
(Italian) A musical notation instructing the musician to slow
the tempo.

roman à clef \roh-mahn ah kley\
(French) A novel that presents a fictionalized account of real
historical people and events.

rondeau \ron-doh\
(French) A courtly love song popular in Medieval and
Renaissance times.

rottweiler \rot-weye-ler\

(German) A breed of dog from the town of Rottweil, where they were known as *Rottweiler Metzgerhunds* "Rottweil butcher-dogs." They were bred to pull butchers' carts.

roué \roo-ey\

(French) A playboy or rake. One who pursues immoral pleasures.

roulette \roo-let\

(French) "Small wheel." A casino game in which a ball is thrown onto a revolving wheel of numbers.

russky \roos-kee\

(Russian) In English, this is sometimes used as a mildly pejorative, slightly comic reference to Russians. It is the kind of word a hardened military leader in a Cold War–era film would use to refer to the crew of the nuclear submarine coming his way. In the Russian language, *russky* is simply how you say "Russian."

sabrage *sah-brahzh*\
(French) Using a saber to remove a champagne cork. Usually done on ceremonial occasions.

sacré bleu *sah-krey bleu*\
(French) This old French, mild curse word is no longer current in its native country but pops up from time to time in ours. It means "sacred blue" and is a substitute for the blasphemous *sacré dieu* or "sacred god." (Blasphemous swearing is considered more offensive in French culture than bodily bad language.)

safari *sah-fahr-ee*\
(Arabic) A journey to witness or hunt animals in their natural habitat, usually in Africa.

salaam alaikum *sah-lahm al-ey-kem*\
(Arabic) A traditional Islamic greeting: "peace upon you." (See page 23.)

salud *sah-lood*\
(Spanish) "Health." Used as a toast.

samizdat \sah-miz-daht\
(Russian) An old Soviet term for an organization that secretly publishes banned literature, and by extension, for the literature itself.

samovar \sam-oh-vahr\
(Russian) A tea urn with a heating device to keep the water at boiling point.

samurai \sa-mu-reye\
(Japanese) A member of an elite Japanese military class.

sanctum sanctorum \sank-tum sank-tor-um\
(Latin) "The holy of holies." The innermost part of a church, temple, or religious shrine, often reserved for clergy.

sang-froid \sang fwah\
(French) "Cold blood." Stoic composure, cool-headedness.

sans \sahnz\
(French) "Without."

sansei \sahn-sey\
(Japanese) A third-generation immigrant from Japan to North America. (*Nisei* is a second-generation immigrant and *issei* is first.)

sans souci *sahn soo-see*\\
(French) Without worry.

santé *sahn-tey*\\
(French) "Health." Used as a toast.

santoor *san-toor*\\
(Arabic) An Indian musical instrument that is stringed and played with mallets, similar to a dulcimer.

sari *sah-ree*\\
(Hindi) A traditional Indian garment worn by women, consisting of a long piece of colorful cotton or silk draped around the body.

sarong *sah-rong*\\
(Malay) A traditional Malaysian garment consisting of a long piece of cloth wrapped around the body.

Sassenach *sas-en-ak*\\
(Scots Gaelic) A Scottish term for an Englishman, the Gaelic word for "Saxon." These days, it is usually used facetiously.

satguru *sat-goo-roo*\\
(Sanskrit) In Hinduism, a wise and highly enlightened *guru*.

satori *sah-tor-ee*\\
(Japanese) Spiritual enlightenment.

satyagraha *saht-yah-grah-hah*\\
(Sanskrit) Pressure for political and social change through nonviolent resistance, as advocated and practiced by Mahatma Gandhi.

savant *sah-vahnt*\\
(French) A person with a great deal of knowledge. It is often applied to someone whose knowledge in one specific, odd area is off the charts compared to his level of knowledge in general. "I am kind of a *savant* about baseball scores."

savoir faire *sav-wahr fer*\\
(French) The instinctive ability to do or say the right thing in any situation.

scenario *sen-ar-ee-oh*\\
(Italian) The plot of a play. It later came to be applied to any hypothetical situation. "Ok, imagine this *scenario*. I ask you out on a date. What do you suppose you'd say?"

schadenfreude *shahd-en-froy-de*\\
(German) Joy in another's misfortune.

MASSACHUSETTS VS. MICHIGAN
THE WORDIEST LATIN STATE MOTTO

MASSACHUSETTS

Ense petit placidam sub libertate quietem. Translation: "By the sword we seek peace, but peace only under liberty."

MICHIGAN

Si quaeris peninsulam amoenam circumspice. Translation: "If you seek a pleasant peninsula, look about you."

THE WINNER?

Michigan. The state's two peninsulas combine to produce a thirty-seven-letter state motto, whereas Massachusetts' peaceful swords only rack up thirty-six. Better luck next time, Bay State.

Honorable mention goes to Missouri for *salus populi suprema lex esto*, "Let the welfare of the people be the supreme law," and Alabama for *audemus jura nostra defendere*, "We dare defend our rights."

schlemiel *shle-meel*\
(Yiddish) An awkward, clumsy bungler.

schlep *shlep*\
(Yiddish) To lug or carry, especially in an awkward manner.

schlimmbesserung *shlim-be-se-rung*\
(German) A so-called improvement that actually makes things worse.

schlong *shlong*\
(German) Slang for the male member.

schlub *shlub*\
(Yiddish) A worthless, unattractive oaf.

schmaltz *shmahlts*\
(Yiddish) Excessive sentimentality.

schmo *shmoh*\
(Yiddish) An idiot. A euphemism for the stronger *schmuck*.

schmuck *shmuk*\
(Yiddish) Slang for the male member. A euphemism for one who behaves in a manner that would make you want to compare him to that organ.

schmutz *shmoots*\\
(German; also Yiddish as *schmuts*) Gunk, as in "you have some *schmutz* on your face."

schnauzer *shnow-zer*\\
(German) "Snouter." A breed of dog with a distinctive bearded snout.

schtick or **shtick** *shtik*\\
(Yiddish) A bit of amusing, usually regularly repeated theatrical material.

schtup or **shtup** *shtoop*\\
(Yiddish) Although the word means "to push" it is more often used as an off-color, but slightly comic, synonym for a good old Anglo Saxon four-letter word for sexual intercourse.

séance *sey-ahns*\\
(French) In the mid-nineteenth century, there was a fashion for spiritualism and mesmerism. At that time this French word for "seat" or "session," which had theretofore been used to describe a meeting in general, came to be applied to people gathering to try to communicate with the dead.

segue \seg-wey\
(Italian) "Follows." It is a bridge connecting one thought or piece of music to another. A frequently used term in broadcasting. "He spoke about how valuable he was to the company before *segue*ing into the issue of his salary."

sehnsucht \zeyn-zookt\
(German) An obscure but useful word meaning "wistful longing."

semper fidelis \sem-per fi-dey-lis\
(Latin) "Always faithful." The motto of the U.S. Marine Corps. Often shortened to *semper fi*.

serape \se-rah-pey\
(Spanish) A long, brightly colored, blanket-like shawl or cape.

serviette \ser-vee-et\
(French) This is a French (and British) way of referring to a table napkin.

shalom \shah-lohm\
(Hebrew) "Peace." A greeting used for both "hello" and "good-bye."

sharia \shah-ree-ah\
(Arabic) Islamic law based on the teachings of the Koran.

Shar-Pei *shar-pey*\

(Cantonese) A dog breed notable for its wrinkled skin and blue-black tongue.

sherpa *sher-pah*\

(Tibetan) In English, the word almost always refers to a mountain-climbing guide. Originally, it referred more broadly to dwellers of the Himalayan region on the borders of Nepal and Tibet, the area where Western climbers hire their sherpas before attempting to summit Mt. Everest.

shiatsu *shee-aht-soo*\

(Japanese) A Japanese therapy similar to acupuncture using the application of pressure on various points of the body, rather than needles.

Shiba Inu *shee-bah ee-noo*\

(Japanese) A breed of dog with thick fur, originally bred for hunting.

shibboleth *shi-boh-leth*\

(Hebrew) Although it is actually an onomatopoetic word for a "stream in flood," it has come down to us as "password" because the ancient Gileadites famously used it as one as a means to identify their enemies who couldn't pronounce the "sh" sound.

A MAD WORLD

Enlish has borrowed a large number of words for madness. Perhaps this has something to do with historic English speakers' views of those "crazy" people from other cultures. Here is a sampling of the world of insane language.

Running "amok" is something frenzied and uncontrollable people do. The word was first used by the Portuguese to describe Malay people who wanted to kill them.

If you're overwhelmed with anxiety you can use the German word *angst* to describe your condition.

When you go "berserk," you are making a reference to a raging Norse warrior via their ancient word *berserkr*.

Delirium is a Latin word for "madness." It is literally a farming metaphor, referring to a plow that has come out of its trough. *Dementia* is another Latin word for "madness." It literally means a person who is "out of his mind." The ancient Romans also used the word *furor* for a more violent, raving madness.

In England, you might hear the slang term "doolally." It takes its name from Deolali, India, the site of a large British military camp in the late-nineteenth century. It was not the Indians who were driven to distraction but the British soldiers who went a bit barmy as they waited there to be sent home.

You can use the Spanish word for crazy, *loco*, and people will know exactly what you mean.

Our word "lunatic" was borrowed from the Old French *lunatique* or "moonsickness."

Mania is what the Greeks called it. Their word is related to a verb meaning "to rage in anger."

The Yiddish *meshuga* has a less clinical and more comic and exasperated connotation.

In the legal profession they turn to Latin for *non compos mentis*, literally "not master of one's mind."

Shih Tzu \shi tsoo\
(Mandarin) A small, *frou-frou* dog with long fur.

shofar \shoh-fahr\
(Hebrew) A Jewish musical horn made from a ram's horn.

shtetl \shte-tel\
(Yiddish) A small Eastern European Jewish town or village.

shul \shool\
(Yiddish) A synagogue.

sic \sik\
(Latin) Used in quoted text to indicate that a mistake was in the original and that the writer doing the quoting was smart enough to recognize it.

sic semper tyrannis \sik sem-per ti-ra-nis\
(Latin) "Thus always to tyrants." These were the words shouted by John Wilkes Booth when he shot Abraham Lincoln. Also the state motto of Virginia.

sic transit gloria mundi
\sik tran-zit glor-ee-ah moon-dee\
(Latin) "Thus passes the glory of the world." A reminder of the transitory nature of earthly life.

sic vita est *sik vee-tah est*\\
(Latin) "Such is life."

sieg heil *zeek hayl*\\
(German) This once meant "hail victory." Now it just means you're a Nazi.

siesta *see-es-tah*\\
(Spanish) An early afternoon nap.

silovik *see-loh-vik*\\
(Russian) A politician with a background in the Soviet military or security services, especially the KGB. The plural is *siloviki*.

simpatico *sim-pah-ti-koh*\\
(Spanish and Italian) Likeable, pleasant to get along with.

sine qua non *see-ney kwah nohn*\\
(Latin) "Without which, nothing." An indispensable condition. "A practical way to travel between the stars is a must-have for space opera, and a *sine qua non* for our frequently vaunted future as a galactic society." —Seth Shostak, American astronomer

Sinn Féin *shin feyn*\\
(Irish Gaelic) The name of the Irish republican movement translates to "we ourselves."

THE SPEED OF SPUTNIK

According to Robert Kraske's *The Story of the Dictionary, Sputnik* is the only word to have been officially welcomed into the English language within twenty-four hours. It happened on October 4, 1957, when the Soviet Union launched the first manmade satellite, *Sputnik I*, into space. An editor in New York saw the word in a headline. He happened to know that the publishing company that owned the newspaper was about to release a new dictionary. He called the office where it was about to be printed, shouted, "Stop the presses!" and dictated a definition of the new word over the phone. One day later, the dictionary was printed, including the word *Sputnik*. *Sputnik*, incidentally, means "fellow traveler" and is the general word Russians use for a satellite. For example, if you set your GPS to speak in Russian and it loses its satellite signal, it will say the Russian word for "lost" followed by *sputniki*.

sitar *si-tar*\\
(Hindi) A guitar-like instrument with a round body.

sláinte *slahn-chah*\\
(Irish Gaelic) A toast to your health.

smorgasbord *smor-gahs-bord*\\
(Swedish) Fans of accent marks take note—here's the word for a large buffet in its native form: *smörgåsbord*.

soi-disant *swah dee-zahn*\\
(French) "Self-named." "So-called." Usually used in derision. "The *soi-disant* professor of economics failed to predict the housing bubble would burst."

soigné *swahn-yey*\\
(French) This French word is popular with foodies who want a more upscale way to say a well-plated meal is "elegant."

soirée *swahr-ey*\\
(French) A party in the evening. As is often the case when a French term is used, the implication is that it will be an elegant, although not formal, affair.

sola gratia *soh-lah grah-tee-ah*\\
(Latin) "By grace alone." The concept that salvation cannot be earned, it is given by God's unmerited favor alone.

sola scriptura *soh-lah skrip-tur-ah*\
(Latin) "By scripture alone." Refers to the idea that the text of the Bible is understandable by the average reader without interpretation by a religious authority, and that the text alone should be the final authority in Christian doctrine. The guiding principle of the Protestant Reformation.

sombrero *som-brer-oh*\
(Spanish) A Mexican hat with a wide brim.

sommelier *som-e-lee-yey*\
(French) A wine waiter. Generally found at an upscale French restaurant rather than, say, an Arby's.

sotto voce *so-toh voh-chey*\
(Italian) In a soft voice.

soubrette *soo-bret*\
(French) A common theatrical character, a lady's maid who is coquettish and sly. Usually a secondary character who sets things in motion for the romantic lead. By extension, any similarly flirtatious and clever young woman.

soupçon *soop-sohn*\
(French) A small amount.

sous-chef \soo-shef\
(French) The second in command in a kitchen. Someone who works under the main chef.

souvenir \soo-ve-neer\
(French) "A memory." More often we use it to mean *tchotchkes* you buy at the gift shop while on vacation.

speculum \spek-yoo-lum\
(Latin) A medical instrument used to examine a passage or cavity of the body. *Speculum* is the Latin word for "mirror" and originally referred to a reflective instrument such as a dental mirror.

spitz \spits\
(German) The small Pomeranian-like dog takes its name from the German word for "pointed," a reference to the shape of its muzzle.

spoor \spoor\
(Afrikaans) The prints and scents an animal leaves behind that allow it to be tracked.

Sputnik \sput-nik\
(Russian) The Russians gave the name "fellow traveler" to their series of satellites and now use it as a generic word for "satellite." (See page 196.)

staccato \stah-kah-toh\

(Italian) In music, notes played in a quick, sharp fashion.

status quo \sta-tus kwoh\

(Latin) The way things are now if nothing changes. (Also an English rock band.)

stet \stet\

(Latin) A printer's proof term used to indicate that a correction should be ignored. This little word means "let it stand."

stigma \stig-mah\

(Latin) A mark of disgrace. The original *stigma* was a brand on the skin made with a hot iron, a Roman way to physically punish and also shame criminals.

stigmata \stig-mah-tah\

(Latin) *Stigmata* is the plural of *stigma*. It is used to refer to the wounds of Christ or wounds like them, which are said to miraculously appear on statues and on some devoted people.

sub judice \sub yoo-di-key\

(Latin) Under consideration by a court but not yet settled.

succès de scandale \suk-sey de skahn-dahl\

(French) Success due to notoriety.

succubus *suk-yoo-bus*\\
(Latin) A female demon who molests men in their sleep. Poor guys. (See page 111.)

sui generis *soo-wee gen-e-ris*\\
(Latin) Unique. One of a kind.

summa cum laude *soo-mah koom low-du*\\
(Latin) "With the highest praise." *Summa cum laude* is higher than *magna cum laude*, which is higher than *cum laude*.

suppressio veri *su-pres-ee-oh ve-ree*\\
(Latin) Most often used in matters of law, this means suppression of the truth.

sutra *soo-trah*\\
(Sanskrit) An aphoristic teaching.

swami *swahm-ee*\\
(Hindi) The word *swami* means "master." It is an honorific given to a Hindu religious teacher.

symposium *sim-pohz-ee-um*\\
(Latin, from the Greek *symposion*) These days, a symposium is a rather dry affair, where experts gather to discuss issues in lecture halls. Back in Greek days, it was a drinking party. The word literally means "drinking together."

tableau vivant *tab-loh vee-vahn*\
(French) A group of living people standing still in the poses of a famous painting. It was a popular parlor game in Victorian England.

taboo *ta-boo*\
(Tongan) Something forbidden or cursed. Spelled *tabu* in Tongan.

tabula rasa *ta-byoo-lah rah-sah*\
(Latin) A clean slate.

tae kwon do *teye kwahn doh*\
(Korean) A Korean martial art with more kicking than *karate*.

t'ai chi *teye chee*\
(Chinese) A martial art consisting of slow movements and controlled balance, and the philosophy behind it.

tamagotchi *ta-ma-got-chee*\
(Japanese) A handheld electronic toy with a digital image of a pet that the owner takes care of by pushing buttons to "feed" it and so on.

tannenbaum *tah-nen-bowm*\\
(German) Christmas tree.

tarantella *tar-an-te-lah*\\
(Italian) A folk dance said to cure tarantula bites.

tatami *tah-tah-mee*\\
(Japanese) A traditional straw mat used as flooring.

tchotchke *choch-kee*\\
(Yiddish) Small objects you have to dust. Knick-knacks.

tempus fugit *tem-pus fyoo-jit*\\
(Latin) Time flies. You often find this inscribed on the dials of old clocks.

terra cognita *ter-ah kog-nee-tah*\\
(Latin) Familiar territory.

terra es, terram ibis *ter-ah es ter-ahm ee-bis*\\
(Latin) "Dust thou art, to dust thou shalt return." A well-known phrase from the book of Genesis in the Latin Vulgate. (The Vulgate is an edition of the Bible that first appeared in print in 1456.)

terra firma *ter-ah fir-mah*\\
(Latin) Dry land.

terra incognita *ter-ah in-kog-nee-tah*\\
(Latin) Unknown territory.

terrazzo *ter-aht-soh*\\
(Italian) A polished flooring material made of marble or
granite in concrete.

tertius gaudens *tur-shee-us gow-dens*\\
(Latin) An obscure but useful term for a "rejoicing third," a
person who fans the flames of emotion because he or she
takes pleasure in seeing two other people argue.

tête à tête *tet ah tet*\\
(French) "Head to head." A face-to-face conversation.

tic douloureux *tik doo-lah-roo*\\
(French) A painful twitch, usually of the facial muscles. In
medicalese: paroxysmal neuralgia.

tiki *tee-kee*\\
(Maori) An image of a human figure, often an ancestor. In
the West, they're used to decorate bars to make them seem
tropical.

tilak *ti-lahk*\\
(Sanskrit) A mark that Hindu people wear on the forehead as
a religious symbol.

FRENCH VS. GERMAN
SLOW-MOVING WIT

L'ESPRIT DE L'ESCALIER

The French came up with the term *l'esprit de l'escalier* to describe a well-known phenomenon. A conversation is finished, the other person is gone, and suddenly into your head pops the cleverest thing you could have said if only you'd thought of it at the time. Well, that's what blogging is for.

TREPPENWITZ

The Germans found this French expression so useful that they created their own version of it. English speakers sometimes adopt the German version for want of a version of our own.

THE WINNER?

As the French came first, they deserve *le grand prix*. That is unless we do like the Germans did and make up our own word. "Stepwit," anyone?

timpani *tim-pah-nee*\
(Italian) A set of kettle drums.

tokus *took-us*\
(Yiddish) A slang word for the part that goes over the fence last. Also spelled *tukhus, tuchis, tuchus, tochis,* or *tuchis,* much as the need to talk about the *derrière* is varied and far-reaching.

torschlusspanik *tor-shloos-pa-nik*\
(German) A sense of angst about the passing of life's opportunities, usually experienced in the middle years.

toupee *too-pey*\
(French) A partial wig or hairpiece used to cover a bald patch.

tour de force *toor de fors*\
(French) An impressive achievement requiring great skill. (There is also a ballet step with this name.)

tout de suite *toot sweet*\
(French) Right away.

tranche de vie *trahnsh de vee*\
(French) A slice of life.

treppenwitz *trep-en vits*\\
(German) The clever rejoinder that comes to mind too late.
The Germans took the French expression *l'esprit de l'escalier*
and made a German word out of it. It means a "staircase
joke." (See page 205.)

triage *tree-ahzh*\\
(French) Sorting of patients so that those with the most
immediate and life-threatening needs can be treated first. Also
applied to any similar attempt to prioritize pressing projects.

troubadour *troo-bah-dor*\\
(French) A traveling poet or singer.

trousseau *troo-soh*\\
(French) Clothes, jewels, and other possessions collected
by the family for the bride for her to take with her when
she marries.

tsetse *set-see* or sometimes *teet-see*\\
(Bantu) A tropical African biting fly.

tsunami *soo-nah-mee*\\
(Japanese) A large wave caused by an earthquake.

tsuris *tsoo-ris*\\
(Yiddish) Serious problems or worries.

TRADITIONAL THANKSGIVING IN MEXICO

Have you ever wondered why the nation Turkey and the bird we stuff at Thanksgiving have the same name? It is no accident. When the English got their first taste of the bird around 1530, it had arrived via Mediterranean traders they called "Turkey merchants" because they came from parts of the Ottoman Empire, meaning they were Turkish. They labeled the unfamiliar fowl a "Turkey cock." Many other Europeans believed the turkey came from India and used a name that translatesd to "India bird." The Danish, Dutch, Finnish, and Norwegians all gave it names that are variants on Calicut, the same Indian port that gave us the word *calico*.

When the Spanish brought the turkey to India via their possessions in the East Indies, they called it the "Peru bird." But the turkey is native to Mexico. Back in the 1520s, Europeans called Mexico "the Spanish Indies" or "the New Indies." This is where all of the confusion began.

tu quoque *too kwoh-kwey*\\

(Latin) In logic, a fallacy in which the speaker tries to win the argument by charging his or her opponent with being a hypocrite and doing the very thing said opponent is arguing against. "You say global warming is real, but you came here on a jet plane, didn't you?"

tycoon *teye-koon*\\

(Japanese) Originally a military leader of imperial Japan, a *tycoon* is now a rich and powerful businessman.

über \oo-ber\

(German) Recently, the German preposition meaning "over" or "above" has entered the lexicon of English slang to indicate something superlative. "That guy is *über* annoying." The Uber ridesharing company began life as "Ubercab," essentially an everywhere cab or "the best cab." For legal reasons, they eventually dropped the *cab* from their name.

über alles \oo-ber ah-lis\

(German) It means "above all" and is usually used in reference to the German anthem *Deutschland über alles*.

uff da \oof dah\

(Norwegian) "Oh there!" An exclamation used in the American Midwest, especially in Minnesota. It expresses a sense of being overwhelmed, similar to the Yiddish *oy vey*. The expression dates back to the nineteenth century and has fallen out of use in its native Norway, but is gaining in popularity in the U.S. (See page 211.)

uhuru \oo-hoo-roo\

(Swahili) "Freedom." The character of Lt. Uhura on *Star Trek* was named after Robert Ruark's novel *Uhuru*.

EXASPERATION INTERNATIONAL

Uff da

This Norwegian phrase has been traveling outward from the land of Minnesota. It flows off the tongue when lifting an object that is heavier than expected, when danger is narrowly averted, or in any context in which you might be tempted to use the Lord's name in vain.

Oy vey

This has a bit more *gravitas* and world-weariness, as well as the comic associations that many Yiddish words convey, thanks to the good work of Jewish comedians. It has the advantage of a long head-start over *uff da*.

The Winner?

When you're handed an astronomical hospital bill in Minneapolis, you might utter an "*uff da*!" If you live closer to New York, the expression is "*oy vey!*" For frequency of use, the Yiddish wins it, *uff da* is gaining. Watch this space.

MEMORATU ETIAM DIGNUM
"ALSO WORTHY OF MENTION"

While researching this book, I came across a number of Latin words and phrases that are not in common use, but maybe they ought to be:

Docendo discitur: Something is learned by teaching.

Furor scribendi: An irresistible urge to write.

Genus irritabile vatum: The irritable race of poets. A phrase used by Horace in his *Epistles*.

Lethologica: The inability to recall the right word.

Lethonomia: The inability to recall the right name.

Hic abundant leones and *hic sunt dracones*: "Here lions abound" and "here be dragons." These were used by mapmakers to mark territories that had not yet been explored. Ripe for metaphorical use.

ukulele \yoo-kah-ley-lee\
(Native Hawaiian) A Hawaiian four-stringed guitar. As if *ukuleles* were not whimsical enough: the name literally means "jumping flea."

ultima ratio \ul-ti-mah rah-tee-oh\
(Latin) The last argument.

umami \oo-mah-mee\
(Japanese) A savory flavor associated with meats, mushrooms, and miso soup.

umlaut \oom-lowt\
(German) Those two little dots over vowels in some foreign words that indicate a change in pronunciation. For example, over the *u* in *über*.

uomo universale \woh-moh yoo-nee-ver-sahl ey\
(Italian) "The universal man." A guy who can do it all. A Renaissance man.

upas \yoo-pas\
(Malay) This tropical Asian tree has a milky juice that is poisonous to humans. The Javanese used it for tipping arrows and use the word *upas* to mean "dart poison." The toxic nature of the plant led to a metaphorical use of the word *upas* as a corrupting or evil influence.

U

ut fata trahunt *oot fah-tah trah-hoont*\

(Latin) "As the fates drag." It means that we have little control over what destiny will bring. *Que sera sera.*

ut infra *oot in-frah*\

(Latin) Scholars use this term instead of "as follows" to show that they are scholarly.

ut supra *oot soo-prah*\

(Latin) Scholars use this term instead of "as previous" to show that they are scholarly.

vade mecum \vah-dey mey-kum\
(Latin) A portable reference book, such as a travel guide.

valet \va-ley\
(French) A man's personal attendant. These are the guys who help the upstairs folk on *Downton Abbey* get dressed.

valise \vah-leez\
(French) A traveling case. The type of thing a valet might carry for you.

vamanos \vah-mah-nohs\
(Spanish) "Let's go!" *Vamos* also means "let's go" and this became, to the ears of people who were not skilled at Spanish, *vamoose* or "get out of here."

varia lectio \vah-ree-ah lek-tee-oh\
(Latin) A scholarly term for a variant reading of a text.

vaya con Dios \vay-yah kon dee-ohs\
(Spanish) "Go with God." The English "good-bye" has a similar connotation, by the way. It's a contraction of "God be with you."

THE PERILS OF BORROWING

VOULEZ-VOUS COUCHER?

If you were looking for a classy way to wrap up a date by directly inviting your would-be *paramour* to, ahem, come upstairs with you, you're probably out of luck. But if you insist upon attempting it, you might try the "Lady Marmalade" approach and say it in French. The song's most famous lyric, "*Voulez-vous coucher avec moi*" means "Do you want to go to bed with me?" It should be noted, however, that the songwriters chose the formal and polite form of "you" for this question, the form reserved for strangers and business associates. One would hope that by the time you're ready to make such a request you will at least be on close enough terms to phrase it *Veux-tu coucher avec moi?*

veld *velt*\
(Afrikaans) Open grasslands in Southern Africa.

vendetta *ven-de-tah*\
(Italian) An ongoing, bitter feud.

veni, vidi, vici *ven-ee, vee-dee, vee-chee*\
(Latin) "I came, I saw, I conquered." The words of Julius Caesar.

venti *ven-tee*\
(Italian) *Venti* is Italian for "twenty" but in one very specific context it means "large." (See page 221.)

verbatim *ver-bey-tim*\
(Latin) Repeating a quote exactly as it was spoken, word for word.

verboten *fer-boh-ten*\
(German) "Forbidden." (Although a *v* in German is pronounced like an English *f*, English speakers usually pronounce the beginning of this word with an English *v*.)

verismo *ver-eez-moh*\
(Italian) Realism. Used to describe literature and theater done in a naturalistic style.

V

vérité \vey-ree-tey\
(French) Truthfulness.

verklempt \fer-klemt\
(Yiddish) Overcome with emotion. Popularized by Mike
Myers on *Saturday Night Live*.

vers de société \ver de soh-see-ey-tey\
(French) "Society verse." Light, witty, and often ironic verse
written for a cultured audience of in-the-know society folks.

vers libre \ver lee-bre\
(French) Free verse.

veto \vee-toh\
(Latin) The right of the president to reject a law takes its name
from the Latin word meaning "I forbid."

via dolorosa \vee-yah doh-loh-roh-sah\
(Latin) "The sorrowful way." Specifically, the journey of Jesus
to his crucifixion.

vibrato \vi-brah-toh\
(Italian) Rapid slight changes in pitch in playing music or
singing.

vice versa \veyes ver-sah\
(Latin) The statements are equally correct when they are
reversed. "He is fond of his dog and *vice versa*."

(la) vida loca \vee-dah loh-kah\
(Spanish) The crazy life.

vide infra \vee-dey in-frah\
(Latin) Academese for "see below."

vide supra \vee-dey soo-prah\
(Latin) Academese for "see above."

(la) vie de Bohème \vee de boh-em\
(French) An unconventional, Bohemian lifestyle. (See
page 223.)

vie en rose \vee ahn rohz\
(French) Life seen through rose-colored glasses.

vigilante \vij-il-an-tee\
(Spanish) *Vigilante* is Spanish for "watchman," but sometimes
in the Old West, the watchman would go above and beyond
and take the law into his own hands.

THE VICHYSSOISE STRATEGY, OR JUST GIVE ME A MEDIUM!

If it is foreign, it must be high quality. At least that is what marketing folks would like you to think. There is a long tradition of companies coming up with pseudo-international names for their products in the hopes that you will part with more money for them.

The *New York Times* coined the term "the vichyssoise strategy" for the practice. Vichyssoise was created at the Ritz Carlton hotel in New York. Thinking their clientele might not respond to "cold potato soup" they invented a name that was suitably French-sounding.

The ersatz Scandinavian luxury ice cream brand Häagen Dazs was invented in the Bronx in 1960 by a Polish immigrant. He put a map of Denmark on his packaging, implying the name is Danish, but it is not. The Danish language doesn't even use an *umlaut*.

In the 1970s, Chrysler's luxury Cordoba had television advertisements featuring actor Ricardo Montalban boasting about the vehicle's "Corinthian leather" seats. The leather did not come from the Greek city of Corinth, nor anywhere else in Europe for that matter. It reportedly came from exotic New Jersey.

Jordache jeans were the creation of a pair of Israeli-born, New York garment makers called the Nakash Brothers. Denim trousers had been workingmen's garments, and in order to position them as an upscale product for the fashion-conscious, the Nakash brothers made up an exotic, French-sounding name, and set off a national craze in the early 1980s for "designer jeans."

The Ginsu knife, a feature of infomercials in the late 1970s and early 1980s, was invented and manufactured in Fremont, Ohio, where it was originally called Quickcut. A team of marketing experts thought it would sell better with an Asian-sounding name that called to mind samurai swords.

If you go into a Starbucks, you are faced with a rather confusing range of coffee sizes. The smallest size has the contradictory label "tall." Next up is "grande," which means "big" in French, Italian, Spanish, and Portuguese. We can infer, perhaps, that it is meant to be Italian by the names of the next two sizes. "Venti," what most restaurants would call large, is Italian for "twenty." It contains twenty ounces of fluid. There is also an extra-large size "trenta," or "thirty."

vignette *vin-yet*\

(French) A small design or sketch, or a short story. Originally, *vignette* was limited to printer's decorations on the sides of book pages, traditionally leaves or vines. (*Vignette* refers to a vineyard.) From there the word was applied to a popular, small mid-nineteenth-century photographic print, and finally to any small, self-contained artwork, including literary.

virtuoso *vir-tyoo-oh-soh*\

(Italian) Someone who is highly skilled in an art, usually a classical one. It can also be used as an adjective: "The dancer gave a *virtuoso* performance."

vis-à-vis *veez-ah-vee*\

(French) "Face to face." In relation to. "We had a heated conversation *vis-à-vis* the time he went *tête à tête* with the *maître d'* over the definition of *al dente*."

viva *vee-vah*\

(Latin) "Long live . . ."

voilà *vwah-lah*\

(French) An exclamation that literally means "See there!" Usually used when someone has just completed a mildly impressive task. "You just put the frosting on the cake and *voilà*! Dessert." (See page 73.)

FRENCH VS. SPANISH
THE WILD LIFE

LA VIE DE BOHÈME

Artistic, nonconformist, free from *bourgeois* constraints.
You are living *la vie de Bohème*. Also, you have that
song from the musical *Rent* to dance to. Ultimately,
Bohème is a geographical reference to the Czech
Kingdom of Bohemia whence the French believed
(wrongly) the gypsies came.

LA VIDA LOCA

Wild and free, dancing the salsa and *merengue* and
drinking margaritas all night, leaving your responsibilities
for *mañana*. You are living *la vida loca*.

THE WINNER?

French nonconformists seem to have more elevated,
artistic tastes than their Spanish counterparts. But the
Spanish crazy life is much more of a party. So crank up the
Ricky Martin track on your stereo, take your clothes off,
and go dancing in the rain.

volte-face \volt fahs\
(French) An about-face, a dramatic change of opinion.

vorlage \for-lah-ge\
(German) "Forward leaning." The position of a skier when he or she leans forward without lifting the heels from the skis.

vorspiel \for-shpeel\
(German) An overture to a musical work or an introductory scene to a play.

vox populi \voks pop-yoo-leye\
(Latin) The voice of the people.

voyeur \voy-yur\
(French) A person who enjoys peeping at others when they are undressed, engaged in sex, or otherwise *inflagrante delicto*.

~W~

wabi-sabi *wah-bee sah-bee*\
(Japanese) An aesthetic based on the beauty of the incomplete and imperfect.

wah gwan *wah gwahn*\
(Jamaican creole) "What's up?" When president Barack Obama went to Jamaica in 2015 he opened a speech with "Greetings massive. *Wah gwan*, Jamaica." It immediately became one of the hottest dance music samples.

wanderjahr *vahn-der-yahr*\
(German) A year in which a person takes off (usually from school) and travels about to gain experience and skills.

wanderlust *wahn-der-lust*\
(German) A desire to wander. Some people have home sickness. A person with *wanderlust* has away sickness.

Weimaraner *way-mar-ah-ner*\
(German) A dog with a distinctive gray coat. Originally from Weimar, Germany.

w

weltanschauung *velt-ahn-shah-wung*\
(German) One's philosophy of life.

weltschmerz *velt-shmertz*\
(German) World weariness. (See page 78.)

wok *wahk*\
(Cantonese) A bowl-shaped metal pan used for frying food at
high temperatures.

wunderbar *voon-der-bahr*\
(German) "Wonderful!"

wunderkind *voon-der-kint*\
(German) A talented young person. A prodigy. (See
page 228.)

WISENHEIMER

It certainly sounds German, but "wisenheimer," meaning a smart aleck, is thoroughly English. It seems that back in the early part of the twentieth century, there was a fad of adding "heimer" to the ends of words to make a comical personal name out of it. (Today someone might make up a name like Tightfist McStingy for the same effect.) H. L. Mencken in *The American Language* published in 1919 noted, "Several years ago "-heimer" had a great vogue in slang, and was rapidly done to death." "Wise-heimer" became "wisen-heimer, and it was the only one of these trendy words to survive."

German vs. French
PRODIGIES

Wunderkind
The German kid is a whiz, talented, awe inspiring; a real wonder.

Enfant Terrible
L'enfant makes up for what he lacks in awesomeness with what you might call marketing. He is a *succès de scandale*. He loves to *épater les bourgeois*. Yet there is something irresistible about him.

The Winner?
The German overachiever seems to be simply marvelous, while the French is precocious at best and mortifying at worst. It looks like the Prussians trump *les Gaulois* this time around.

yahrzeit \yar-zeyet\
(German) The anniversary of the death of a loved one, especially a parent.

yakuza \yah-koo-zah\
(Japanese) A Japanese gangster.

yang \yang\
(Chinese) The masculine principle of the two complimentary forces of the universe. (See also *yin*.)

yaoi \yah-oh-ee\
(Japanese) A genre of *manga* also known as "boys' love." They depict same-sex romances between male characters but are mostly written by women for a female audience.

yarmulke \yahr-mul-kah\
(Yiddish) A head-covering worn by Jewish men during prayer.

yashmak \yash-mak\
(Turkish) A face covering worn by Muslim women, usually with a *chador*.

German vs. French
FABULOUSLY FULL-FIGURED

EMBONPOINT

In an era in which our idea of physical perfection is a size-zero fashion model, this French expression meaning "plump and chubby in a way that indicates good health" has largely fallen out of use, but it deserves to be revived. It literally means "in good condition."

ZAFTIG

Meanwhile, this German word for a woman who is curvy and rounded in all the right places is gaining prominence.

THE WINNER?

Embonpoint hints at an entire way of viewing a healthy lifestyle. You can imagine the full-figured French *femme* enjoying long meals with good company, wrapping up a meal with guilt-free enjoyment of delicious cheeses and wine.

But the full-figured *fräulein* is much more sassy and sexy. The *zaftig* woman merits a va-va-voom. So on behalf of all of the larger ladies, I award this one to the Germans.

yenta \yen-tah\
(Yiddish) A female busybody and gossip.

yin \yin\
(Chinese) The feminine principle of the two complimentary forces of the universe. (See also *yang*.)

yoga \yoh-gah\
(Sanskrit) A Hindu spiritual discipline which incorporates meditation, controlled body postures, and breathing.

yogi \yoh-gee\
(Sanskrit) A man who practices yoga.

yogini \yoh-gee-nee\
(Sanskrit) A woman who practices yoga.

yucca \yuk-ah\
(Spanish) A perennial shrub native to Mexico and South America.

yurt \yurt\
(Russian) A circular fur or skin tent used by nomads in Siberia, Mongolia, and Turkey.

zaftig *zahf-tig*\\
(German) Curvy. Slightly plump in a pleasing, attractive way.
(See page 230).

zeitgeist *zeyet-geyest*\\
(German) The general feeling and mentality of a given era
in time.

zendo *zen-doh*\\
(Japanese) A room set aside for Zen Buddhist meditation.

zeppelin *zep-lin*\\
(German) An airship. Named for Count Ferdinand von
Zeppelin.

zori *zoh-ree*\\
(Japanese) A straw or rubber sandal with a thong between
the toes. Similar to flip-flops.

zucchetto *zoo-ke-toh*\\
(Italian) A brimless cap, similar to a *yarmulke*, worn by
members of certain Catholic orders.

Mock Italian (Sort Of)
ZAMBONI

The Zamboni, a machine that resurfaces the ice in a skating rink, is not an Italian loanword. It was invented and named right here in the United States. That said, Frank Zamboni, its inventor, was the son of Italian immigrants. Zamboni worked in the ice business in California back in the days when people kept their food cold in ice boxes. By the 1930s, refrigerators were starting to eliminate the need for homes to buy big blocks of ice. In response to this technological change, Zamboni decided to open an ice rink. The one task he hated was resurfacing the ice. It took about an hour and a half to do with a planer, brushes, and hoses. So Zamboni invented a vehicle a bit like a tractor that could streamline the task. It made it possible to spend more time skating and playing hockey, and less time preparing the ice. But the reason hockey fans love to talk about the Zamboni is that the name is so fun to say.

MOCK MAORI

Finally, for lovers of the fin-de-alphabet, there is *zzxjoanw*, which still shows up in reference books from time to time as a Maori word for a musical instrument, either a fife or a drum. *Zzxjoanw* made its first literary appearance in Rupert Hughes's *The Musical Guide*, published in 1903 and reprinted in 1912 and 1939. Hughes indicated that the word should be pronounced "shaw." Although it gained currency in books on odd words, if not in general parlance, *zzxjoanw* was a *canard*. As Ross Eckler wrote in *Making the Alphabet Dance*, "A hoax clearly entered somewhere; no doubt Hughes expected it to be obvious, but he did not take into account the credulity of logologists."

zugzwang *zug-zvang*\

(German) A state of play in chess where any move will put the player at a disadvantage.

zwischenzug *zvi-shen-tsook*\

(German) Used in the game of chess, it refers to an "intermediate move," in which a player, before executing an expected move, first completes another move that puts the opponent at a disadvantage.

RESOURCES

BOOKS

Archer, Peter, and Linda Archer. *500 Foreign Words & Phrases You Should Know to Sound Smart*. Avon, MA: Adams Media, 2012.

Buchanan-Brown, John, et al., eds. *Le Mot Juste: A Dictionary of Classical and Foreign Words and Phrases*. New York: Vintage Books, 1991.

Delahunty, Andrew. *Oxford Dictionary of Foreign Words and Phrases*. Oxford: Oxford University Press, 1992.

Durkin, Philip. *Borrowed Words*. Oxford: Oxford University Press, 2014.

Ehrlich, Eugene. *Amo, Amas, Amat and More: How to Use Latin to Your Own Advantage and to the Astonishment of Others*. New York: Harper Row, 1985.

———, ed. *The Harper Dictionary of Foreign Terms*. New York: Harper and Row, 1987.

Haubrich, William S. *Medical Meanings. A Glossary of Word Origins*. Philadelphia, PA. American College of Physicians, 1997.

Hendrickson, Robert. *Ladybugs, Tiger Lilies & Wallflowers: A Gardener's Book of Words*. New York: Prentice Hall, 1993.

———. *QPB Encyclopedia of Word and Phrase Origins*. New York: Facts on File, 1997.

Manser, Martin H. *Facts on File Dictionary of Foreign Words and Phrases*. New York: Facts on File, 2008.

McCrum, Robert, et al. *The Story of English*. New York: Viking, 1986.

Rees, Nigel. *Cassell's Dictionary of Word and Phrase Origins*. London: Cassell, 1996.

Room, Adrian. *Cassell's Dictionary of Foreign Words and Phrases*. London: Cassell, 2000.

Sherk, William. *500 Years of New Words*. Doubleday: Garden City, NY, 1983.

Tuleja, Tad. *Foreignisms*. New York: Macmillan, 1989.

Urdang, Lawrence, et al., eds. *Loanwords Dictionary*. Detroit: Gale Research, 1988.

Varchaver, Mary, and Frank Ledlie Moore. *The Browser's Dictionary of Foreign Words and Phrases*. Edison, NJ: Castle Books, 2006.

Vincent, Norah, and Chad Conway. *The Instant Intellectual: The Quick and Easy Guide to Sounding Smart and Cultured*. New York: Hyperion, 1998.

WEBSITES

ATLA Language Services http://www.altalang.com/beyond-words/

Language Log http://languagelog.ldc.upenn.edu/nll/

OneLook Dictionary Search http://www.onelook.com/

Online Etymology Dictionary http://www.etymonline.com/

World Wide Words http://www.worldwidewords.org/

SPECIFIC SOURCES

http://www.csmonitor.com/World/Security-Watch/
Backchannels/2014/0506/Boko-Haram-doesn-t-really-
mean-Western-education-is-a-sin

On objections to the use of the word *haboob*: http://langua-
gelog.ldc.upenn.edu/nll/?p=3295

On OK: http://www.bbc.com/news/magazine-12503686

On *que sera sera*: http://mypage.siu.edu/lhartman/kss/
quesera1.html

ABOUT THE AUTHOR

Laura Lee is the author of fifteen books with such publishers as Harper Collins, Reader's Digest, Lyons Press, and Running Press. She is best known for humorous reference such as *The Pocket Encyclopedia of Aggravation*, which sold 85,000 copies for Black Dog and Leventhal. The *San Francisco Chronicle* has said of her work: "Lee's dry, humorous tone makes her a charming companion. . . . She has a penchant for wordplay that is irresistible."

After a three-year stint as a part-time touring public relations director for a Russian ballet company, Laura has returned to her native Michigan where she divides her time between writing and producing ballet educational tours with Russian ballet star Valery Lantratov.